Tatting with Anne Orr

by ANNE ORR

DOVER PUBLICATIONS, INC., NEW YORK

Published in Canada by General Publishing Company, Ltd., 30 Lesmill Road, Don Mills, Toronto, Ontario.
Published in the United Kingdom by Constable and Company, Ltd., 10 Orange Street, London WC2H 7EG.

This Dover edition, first published in 1989, is an altered and abridged republication of *Tatting, Book No. 13*, published by Anne Orr, Nashville, Tennessee, n.d., and the *Star Book of Tatting Designs, Book No. 2*, published by the American Thread Company, New York, in 1935. The patterns from the two books have been combined and rearranged. The photograph of and instructions for one item and the sections "Abbreviations in Tatting," "Note," "How to Make Tatting" and "List of Anne Orr Publications" have been omitted from *Tatting, Book No. 13*, and several items have been renumbered. The photograph of and instructions for one item, and two additional photographs, have been omitted from the *Star Book of Tatting Designs*. A new Introduction has been written specially for this edition.

Manufactured in the United States of America
Dover Publications, Inc., 31 East 2nd Street, Mineola, N.Y. 11501

Library of Congress Cataloging-in-Publication Data

Orr, Anne Champe.
    Tatting with Anne Orr / by Anne Orr.
      p.   cm.—(Dover needlework series)
    "Altered and abridged republication of Tatting, book no. 13 . . . n.d. and the Star book of tatting designs, book no. 2, published . . . in 1935"—T.p. verso.
      ISBN 0-486-25982-X
    1. Tatting—Patterns. I. Title. II. Series.
TT840.T38077   1989
746.43'6041—dc19
                                      88-34326
                                      CIP

Introduction

During her long career, Anne Orr became one of the most popular needlework designers of her time, and still remains today, more than forty years after her death, one of the best-known names in the needlework field. During the years between 1914 and 1945, she prepared almost a hundred books of needlework designs, and, in addition, served as needlework editor of *Good Housekeeping* magazine for over twenty years. She was proficient in all forms of needlework, creating designs for embroidery, quilting, knitting, crocheting and, of course, tatting. In this, our ninth collection of Anne Orr's patterns and our second collection of her tatting designs, we offer instructions for doilies, luncheon sets, collars, yokes, baby bonnets, 40 separate medallions and over 50 edgings.

While the specific threads mentioned in the instructions may no longer be available, other threads can easily be substituted. Threads made specifically for tatting are available and any smooth cotton thread used for fine crochet can also be used for tatting. The thread numbers used in the instructions to indicate the thread size are the same as those used today, so choosing a suitable thread should present no problem.

Instructions for Tatting

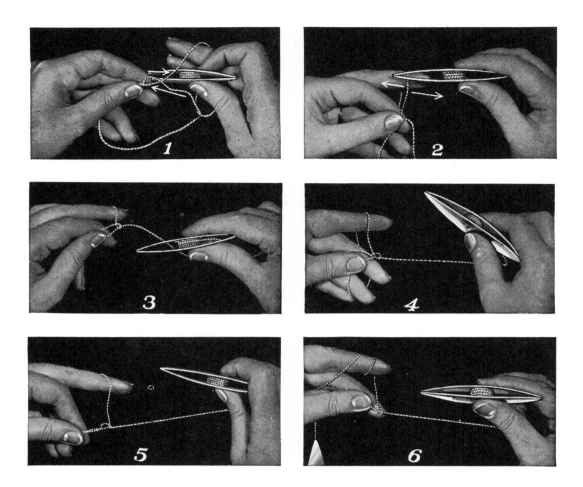

Tatting is a form of lace made with a tatting shuttle, and for some designs only one shuttle is needed, while for others two are required.

As will be judged, the simplest form of tatting is the ring which is made with one shuttle, and when a chain is introduced, the second shuttle is required. In learning to tat, the knot is made on the shuttle thread, and not with it though all the action is taken with the shuttle thread, shown in illustration No. 3. A second important fact to remember is that the shuttle thread is pulled taut before the knot is tightened.

First, wind the thread around the bobbin in the shuttle, layer over layer, but the thread should never extend over the edge.

To make a ring: Hold the shuttle between the thumb and forefinger of the right hand as shown. Hold the end of the thread between the thumb and forefinger of the left hand and pass it around the fingers of this hand, not too tightly, crossing it under the thumb. It is with this loop of thread that the ring is worked and this is called the ring thread. Throw the shuttle thread over the right hand as in illustration No. 1. Pass the shuttle between the first and second fingers of left hand under the shuttle and ring threads and back over ring thread, allowing the ring thread to fall slack by bringing the four fingers of the left hand together. Pull shuttle thread taut, then open the fingers of the left hand until the loop is caught with the thumb, as shown in No. 3.

For the second half, the thread is dropped instead of raised, shuttle is passed over the left-hand thread instead of under (as before), is brought through below between the two threads (as before) and drawn up in the same way. (Illustration No. 2.) Illustration No. 4 shows the second half of stitch slipping into place beside the first half.

This group is called a double stitch and is the main stitch used in tatting. In making this, it will be found that by pulling the shuttle thread and then the ring thread, the stitch slips back and forth on the shuttle thread. If it does not, the stitch has been locked and must be made over again.

Illustration No. 5 shows a picot which is made by leaving a space of thread between the stitches, and to join two picots, draw the working thread through the picot and pass shuttle through loop. Then draw up close to resemble a half stitch, but not to be counted as one.

Two shuttles are required to make a design having a chain. Tie the threads together and hold between the thumb and second finger of the left hand and with the first finger outstretched, wind the thread around it two or three times, allowing the second shuttle to drop as on No. 6. The stitches for the chain are made with the thread between the first and second fingers in the same way as those for the rings.

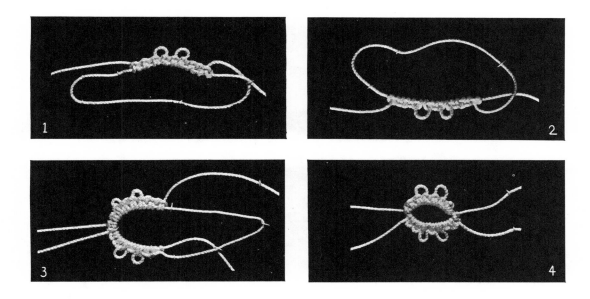

DIRECTIONS FOR THE REVERSE STITCH

Begin ring, making three double stitches, picot, two double stitches, picot, three double stitches (figure one) (this is one-half of ring), take work off from hand* (reverse), turn over (figure two), put work on hand so that the thread which was under is now over the hand. Take shuttle No. 2 and make the other half of the ring, with the reverse stitch, which is done by holding the thread on the hand taut, and making the stitch with the thread from the shuttle, making three double stitches, picot, two double stitches, picot, three double stitches (figure three), take work from hand, turn over*, take shuttle No. 1 and close ring (figure four).

In joining while doing reverse work, do not draw shuttle very taut after passing through joining loop, but draw the loop back again so that the joining stitch is made with the thread from shuttle and the thread on the hand may be drawn back and forth.

ABBREVIATIONS IN TATTING

r st—Stands for reverse stitch.
sl st—Stands for slip stitch.
ds—Stands for double stitch.
r—Stands for ring.
p—Stands for picot.
ch—Stands for chain.

s ch—Stands for short chain.
l ch—Stands for long chain.
lp—Stands for long picot.
j—Stands for join, joined, joining.
sp—Stands for space.
cl—Stands for close.

sep—Stands for separated.
p ch—Stands for picot chain.
lr—Stands for large ring.
sr—Stands for small ring.
lp ch—Stands for long picot chain.
sk—skip.

NOTES

All beginners should use coarse thread to see work better.

Never break off thread after winding shuttle if directions call for chain (ch).

When a shuttle has a point or hook, be careful to keep point forward.

Rings are to be made close together unless directions call for space (sp).

A ring is always to be drawn close unless otherwise stated.

Space means to allow thread between last ring and new one.

When making medallions, doilies, or centerpieces, the work will be lovelier and easier to do if it is pressed every two or three rows, in the desired form, and to do this place on a thick pad, shape, and press over a damp cloth, and then a dry one, until the piece is dry. This will show how the work is going, and will keep from being too full or too tight.

Medallion Centerpiece

Crochet Cotton No. 30.

CENTER—8 r of 3 p, sep by 3 ds, leaving ⅜ inch sp, j each new r to preceding r by 1st p and j last r to 1st r, cl—tie and cut.

1st Row—R 6 ds, j to p of center, 6 ds, cl—ch 3 p, sep by 3 ds—rep 1st row around, tie and cut.

2d Row—Sr 3 p sep by 4 ds, j center p to 1st p of ch, last row, cl—sp (¾ inch)—turn—lr, 6 ds, 7 p, sep by 2 ds, 6 ds, cl—sp as before—rep around, j sr to p of 1st row and to each preceding sr; j lr to each preceding lr by 1st p, j last lr to 1st lr made—tie and cut. Fit medallions around piece of any shape and fasten together by tying with fine sewing thread.

Lunch Cloth and Doily

Lunch Cloth

Crochet Cotton No. 15.

SQUARE MEDALLION—Center R—1 ds, 8 p, sep by 2 ds, 1 ds, cl—tie and cut.

1st Row—1st lr, 5 p, sep by 5 ds, cl—ch 3 ds, j to p of center r, 3 ds—turn—sr 5 ds, j to p of preceding lr, 2 p, sep by 5 ds, cl—rep ch—rep from 1st lr around, j each r to preceding r by 1st p; and j last r to 1st r—tie and cut—J medallions as illustrated. Make 6 squares for each corner.

HALF SQUARES—Rep square medallion, tying after 3rd lr. Make 4 half squares.

EDGE—R, 3 p, sep by 4 ds, cl—ch 3 ds, 3 p, sep by 1 ds, 3 ds—rep edge around, j each new r to preceding r, and to p of corner, tie and cut.

Small Doily Edge

Crochet Cotton No. 50.

1st Row—Sr 2 ds, p, 2 ds, cl—ch 2 ds, p, 2 ds—repeat to desired length. If doily is crocheted around this row may be easily j by p of ch to edge of piece.

2d Row—1st lr, 8 ds, p, 5 ds, j to p of sr, 4 ds, cl—rep lr, (read backwards) j 2nd j to next sr—ch 3 ds, 10 p, sep by 1 ds, 3 ds—rep 1st lr, j 1st p to p of preceding lr, and 2nd p to next sr—rep 2nd row around, tie and cut.

Large Centerpiece

(Continued on page 10)

(Two Shuttles)

The large centerpiece shown on the table on pages 12 and 13 may be made of either SILKINE CROCHET COTTON or STAR CROCHET COTTON, in Size 40, and requires about 5 balls of this size.

R 18 lp, cl. Tie and cut.

1st row: Lr 3 ds, 7 p, 3 ds, cl, *turn, sp (¼-inch), sr 3 ds, j to p of center r, 3 ds, cl, turn, sp, lr 3 ds, j to seventh p of last lr, 6 p, 3 ds, cl. Repeat from * around. Join to first lr. Tie and cut. **2d row:** R 3 ds, p, 2 ds, j to center p of lr (last row), 2 ds, p, 3 ds, cl, turn, sp, r 3 ds, 3 p sep by 3 ds, 3 ds, cl, *(turn, sp, r 3 ds, j to third p of opposite r, 2 ds, j to third p of lr (last row), 2 ds, p, 3 ds, cl, turn, sp, lr 3 ds, j to third p of opposite r, 10 p, 3 ds, cl, turn, sp, r 3 ds, j to third p of opposite r, 2 ds, sk 1 p of same lr (last row), j to next p, 2 ds,

p, 3 ds, cl, turn, sp, r 3 ds, j to eleventh p of last lr, 3 ds, 2 p sep by 3 ds, 3 ds, cl) 3 times, turn, sp, r 3 ds, j to p of opposite r, 2 ds, j to center p of next lr (last row), 2 ds, p, 3 ds, cl, turn, sp, r 3 ds, j to eleventh p of last lr, 3 ds, 2 p sep by 3 ds, 2 ds, cl. Repeat from * around, j round. Tie and cut.

3d row: R 3 ds, 3 p sep by 3 ds, 3 ds, cl, turn, sp, r 3 ds, p, *3 ds, j to center p of lr (last row), 3 ds, p, 3 ds, cl, (turn, sp, r 3 ds, j to third p of opposite r, 3 ds, 2 p sep by 3 ds, 3 ds, cl, turn, sp, r 3 ds, j to third p of opposite r, 3 ds, 2 p sep by 3 ds, 3 ds, cl) 2 times, turn, sp, r 3 ds, j to third p of opposite r, 3 ds, 2 p sep by 3 ds, 3 ds, cl, turn, sp, r 3 ds, j to third p of opposite r, repeat from * around. Join round. Tie and cut.

4th row: Join thread to a p of last row. *Ch 4 ds, p, 4 ds, j in next p (last row), repeat from *. Join, tie and cut.

Round Doily Set

Directions on page 10

Round Doily Set

Illustrated on page 9

The three doilies are made of No. 50 SILKINE CROCHET COTTON, or STAR CROCHET COTTON, and approximately 4 balls of either cotton are needed for the large doily, 2 balls for the medium size, and 2 balls for the small one.

SMALL TATTED DOILY

(7-inch)

Two shuttles.

Center: Lr 7 ds, 6 p sep by 3 ds, 7 ds, cl, (lr 7 ds, j to sixth p of last r, 3 ds, 5 p sep by 3 ds, 7 ds, cl) 3 times. Join last r to first r. Tie and cut.

1st row: *R 4 ds, j to a p of lr, 4 ds, cl, turn, ch 5 ds, p 5 ds, turn. Repeat from * around. Tie and cut.

2d row: *Sr 3 ds, 3 p sep by 3 ds, 3 ds, cl, lr, 3 ds, j to third p of last r, 3 ds, p, 3 ds, j to p of ch over center of lr of center, 3 ds, 2 p sep by 3 ds, 3 ds, cl, sr 3 ds, j to fifth p of lr, 3 ds, 2 p sep by 3 ds, 3 ds, cl, (turn, ch 5 ds, 3 p sep by 2 ds, 5 ds, turn, r 3 ds, 3 p, 3 ds, j to next p (last row), 3 ds, p, 3 ds, cl) 3 times. Turn, ch 5 ds, 3 p sep by 2 ds, 5 ds. Repeat from * around. Tie and cut.

3d row: *R 4 p, j to center p of ch (last row), 4 p, cl, turn, ch 5 ds, 5 p sep by 2 ds, 5 ds, turn, r 4 p, j to first p of next ch, 4 p, cl, turn, ch 5 ds, 5 p sep by 2 ds, 5 ds, turn, r 4 p, j to third p of same ch, 4 p, cl, turn, ch 5 ds, 5 p sep by 2 ds, 5 ds, turn. Repeat from * around. Tie and cut.

4th row: *Sr 4 ds, p 4 ds, cl, lr 4 ds, j to p of sr, 4 ds, j to center p of ch (last row), 4 ds, p, 4 ds, cl, sr, 4 ds, j to third p of lr, 4 ds, cl, turn, ch 6 ds, 5 p sep by 2 ds, 5 ds, turn. Repeat from * around. Tie and cut.

5th row: Sr 2 ds, p, 2 ds, j to center p of ch (last row), 2 ds, p, 2 ds, cl, *turn, ch 5 ds, p, 5 ds, turn, r 2 ds, p, 2 ds, j to third p of last r, 2 ds, p, 2 ds, cl, r 2 ds, 3 p sep by 2 ds, 2 ds, cl, turn, ch 5 ds, 5 p, 5 ds, turn, r 2 ds, j to center p of last r, 2 ds, j to center p of next ch, 2 ds, p, 2 ds, cl. Repeat from * around. Tie and cut.

6th row: *R 9 p, cl, turn, ch 5 ds, 2 p sep by 2 ds, 2 ds, j to p of ch (last row), 2 ds, 2 p sep by 2 ds, 5 ds, turn. Repeat from * around. Tie and cut.

7th row: *R 2 p, j to seventh p of r (last row), 3 p, j to third p of next r, 2 p, cl, turn, ch 5 ds, 5 p sep by 2 ds, 5 ds, turn. Repeat from * around. Tie and cut.

MEDIUM SIZE DOILY

(8½-inch)

Repeat the center and first five rows of Small Doily.
Make 12 motifs as follows:

Center: R 7 ds, 5 p sep by 3 ds, 7 ds, cl, (r 7 ds, j to fifth p of last r, 3 ds, 4 p sep by 3 ds, 7 ds, cl) 3 times. Join last r to first r. Tie and cut.

*R 3 ds, p, 3 ds, j to second p of lr (in center), 3 ds, p, 3 ds, cl, turn, ch 5 ds, 3 p sep by 2 ds, 5 ds, turn, sr 3 ds, 3 p sep by 3 ds, 3 ds, cl, lr 3 ds, j to third p of sr, 3 ds, p, 3 ds, j to next p of same lr, 3 ds, 2 p sep by 3 ds, 3 ds, cl, sr 3 ds, j to fifth p of lr, 3 ds, 2 p sep by 3 ds, 3 ds, cl, turn, ch 5 ds, 3 p sep by 2 ds, 5 ds, turn, r 3 ds, 3 p, 3 ds, j to next p of same lr, 3 ds, p, 3 ds, cl, turn, ch 5 ds, 3 p sep by 2 ds, 5 ds, turn. Repeat from * around. (Join center p of ch between the r and shamrock to center p of ch of last row, and the center p of ch between the same shamrock and next r, to the center p of next ch of last row.) Tie and cut.
Join the next motif to last motif in like manner. Skip 2 ch last row between each motif.

LARGE DOILY

(16-inch)

Repeat the Small Doily.

8th row: Lr 2 ds, 2 p sep by 2 ds, 2 ds, j to center p of ch (last row), 2 ds, 2 p sep by 2 ds, 2 ds, cl, *(turn, ch 4 ds, sr 3 ds, p, 3 ds, cl, r 3 ds, p, 3 ds, cl) 2 times, turn, ch 4 ds, turn, lr 2 ds, 5 p sep by 2 ds, 2 ds, cl, (turn, ch 4 ds, sr 3 ds, p, 3 ds, cl, r 3 ds, p, 3 ds, cl) 2 times, turn, ch 4 ds, turn, r 2 ds, 2 p sep by 2 ds, 2 ds, sk 1 ch, j to center p of next ch, 2 ds, 2 p sep by 2 ds, 2 ds, cl. Repeat from * around. Tie and cut.

9th row: Make like sixth row, allowing 2 ch between the 2 lr of last row. Join center p of next ch to center p of lr.

10th row: Repeat seventh row.
Make 18 motifs, using the center and first two rows of small doily. Join together by the center p of the 2 ch in corner and join each to last row, as for medium size doily.

LARGE CENTERPIECE

(Continued from page 8)

5th row: Repeat fourth row.
6th row—Small Motif—*R 4 ds, p, 4 ds, j to p of ch (last row), 4 ds, p, cl, (r 4 ds, j to third p of last r, 4 ds, 2 p sep by 4 ds, 4 ds, cl) 3 times, j fourth r to first r. Tie and cut. Repeat from *, sk 1 p (last row), j next motif to next p, and j second p of second r to p of last motif.

7th row: *Sr 3 ds, p, 3 ds, cl, turn, sp, r 3 ds, p, 3 ds, j to p (last row), 3 ds, p, 3 ds, cl, turn, sp, sr 3 ds, j to p of last sr, 3 ds, cl, turn, sp, r 3 ds, j to third p of opposite r, 3 ds, 2 p sep by 3 ds, 3 ds, cl, turn, sp, sr, 3 ds, p, 3 ds, cl, turn, sp, r 3 ds, j to third p of opposite r, 3 ds, 2 p sep by 3 ds, 3 ds, cl, turn, sp, repeat from * around. Tie and cut.

8th row: Make like seventh row, j 1 sr to p with the 2 sr, and 2 sr with the 1 sr.

9th row: R 3 ds, 3 p sep by 3 ds, 3 ds, cl, turn, sp, r 3 ds, p, 3 ds, j to p (last row), 3 ds, p, 3 ds, cl, turn, sp, *lr 3 ds, j to third p of opposite r, 8 p, 3 ds, cl, turn, sp, r 3 ds, j to opposite r, 3 ds, j to p (last row), 3 ds, p, 3 ds, cl, turn, sp, r 3 ds, j to ninth p of lr, 3 ds, 2 p sep by 3 ds, 3 ds, cl, turn, sp, r 3 ds, j to p of opposite r, 3 ds, j to next p (last row), 3 ds, p, 3 ds, cl, repeat from * around. Join round, tie and cut.

10th row: Like sixth row, j small motifs to center p of lr (last row).
Make Large Motifs around edge as follows: R 12 p, cl. Tie and cut.

1st row: Lr 3 ds, 7 p, 3 ds, cl, *turn, sp, sr 3 ds, j to p of center r, 3 ds, cl, turn, sp, lr 3 ds, j to seventh p of last lr, 6 p, 3 ds, cl, repeat from * around. Join to first lr. Tie and cut.

2d row: Lr 3 ds, 5 p, j to p of small motif (last row), 5 p, 3 ds, cl, turn, sp, r 3 ds, p, 3 ds, *j to third p of lr (last row), 3 ds, p, 3 ds, cl, turn, sp, r 3 ds, j to eleventh p of last lr, 3 ds, 2 p sep by 3 ds, 3 ds, cl, turn, sp, r 3 ds, j to p of opposite r, 3 ds, j to fifth p of same lr (last row), 3 ds, p, 3 ds, cl, turn, sp lr, 3 ds, j to p of opposite r, 4 p, j to p of next small motif, 5 p, 3 ds, cl, turn, sp, r 3 ds, j to p of opposite r, 3 ds, j to third p of lr (last row), 3 ds, p, 3 ds, cl, turn, sp, r 3 ds, j to eleventh p of last lr, 3 ds, 2 p sep by 3 ds, 3 ds, cl, turn, sp, r 3 ds, j to third p of opposite r, 3 ds, j to fifth p of same lr (last row), 3 ds, p, 3 ds, cl, turn, sp, lr 3 ds, j to third p of opposite r, 4 p, j to p of next small motif, 5 p, 3 ds, cl, *turn, sp, r 3 ds, j to third p of lr (last row), 3 ds, p, 3 ds, cl, turn, sp, r 3 ds, j to eleventh p of last lr, 3 ds, 2 p sep by 3 ds, 3 ds, cl, turn, sp, r 3 ds, j to p of opposite r, 3 ds, j to fifth p of same lr (last row), 3 ds, p, 3 ds, cl, turn, sp, lr 3 ds, j to p of opposite r, 10 p, 3 ds, cl. Repeat from * around. Tie and cut. Make other motifs, j together by center p of 2 lr.

Make a lr and j between the large motifs on both sides of the motifs, as follows: R 4 ds, j to p of sr, 9 p, j to p of sr of next motif, 4 ds, cl. Tie and cut.

Baby Caps

These two attractive baby caps may be made of either SILKINE CROCHET COTTON or STAR CROCHET COTTON, in size 70, or of SILKINE TATTING COTTON, and two shuttles, and 3 balls for each are required.

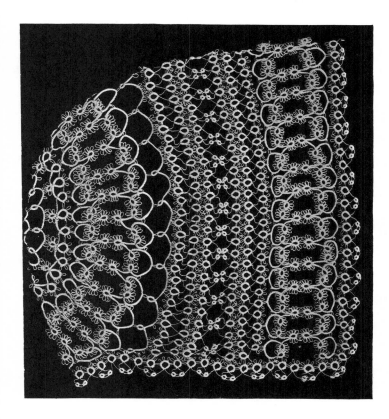

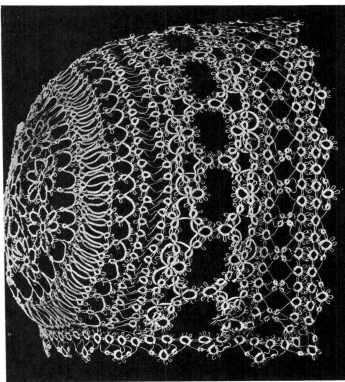

THE UPPER CAP

Center: R 13 lp, cl. **1st row:** *R 3 ds, j to p of center r, 3 ds, cl, turn, ch 6 ds, p, 6 ds, turn, repeat from * around. Tie and cut. **2d row:** *R 4 ds, j to p of ch (last row) 4 ds, cl, turn, ch 5 ds, 3 p sep by 2 ds, 5 ds, turn, repeat from * around. Tie and cut. **3d row:** R 5 ds, 5 p sep by 2 ds, 5 ds, cl, *r 2 ds, 3 p, j to center p of ch (last row), 3 p, 2 ds, cl, turn, ch 7 ds, turn, r 5 ds, j in fifth p of opposite r, 2 ds, 4 p sep by 2 ds, 5 ds, cl, turn, ch 7 ds, turn, r 5 ds, j in fifth p of last r, 2 ds, 4 p sep by 2 ds, 5 ds, cl, repeat from * around. Tie and cut. **4th row:** R 9 p, cl, turn, ch 7 ds, p, 7 ds, j to center p of r (last row), 7 ds, p, 7 ds, *r 4 p, j to center p of last r, 4 p, cl, (turn, ch 7 ds, turn, r 9 p, cl) twice, turn, ch 7 ds, j to p of opposite ch, 7 ds, j to center p of next r (last row), 7 ds, p, 7 ds, repeat from * around. Tie and cut. **5th row:** R 9 p, cl, turn, ch 7 ds, *(p, 9 ds, turn, p, 7 ds, turn, r 4 p, j to center p of last r, 4 p, cl, turn, ch 7 ds, turn, r 4 p, j to center p of r (last row), 4 p, cl, turn, ch 7 ds, turn, r 9 p, cl, turn, ch 7 ds, j to p of opposite ch, repeat from * around. Tie and cut. **6th row:** *R 4 ds, j to p of ch (last row), 4 ds, cl, turn, ch 8 ds, 5 p sep by 2 ds, 8 ds, turn, repeat from * around with exception of last 4 p of last row. Tie and cut. **7th row:** R 4 ds, 2 p sep by 2 ds, 2 ds, j to second p of ch (last row), 2 ds, 2 p sep by 2 ds, 4 ds, cl, turn, sp (¼-inch), r 4 ds, 5 p sep by 2 ds, 4 ds, cl, *turn, sp, r 4 ds, j to fifth p of opposite r, 2 ds, p, 2 ds, sk 1 p on ch, (last row), j in next p, 2 ds, 2 p sep by 2 ds, 4 ds, cl, turn, sp, r 4 ds, j to fifth p of opposite r, 2 ds, 4 p sep by 2 ds, 4 ds, cl, turn, sp, r 4 ds, j to fifth p of opposite r, 2 ds, 4 p sep by 2 ds, 4 ds, cl, turn, sp, r 4 ds, j to fifth p of opposite r, 2 ds, 4 p sep by 2 ds, 4 ds, cl, turn, sp, r 4 ds, j to fifth p of opposite r, 2 ds, p, 2 ds, j to second p of next ch, 2 ds, 2 p sep by 2 ds, 4 ds, cl, turn, sp, r 4 ds, j to p of opposite r, 2 ds, 4 p sep by 2 ds, 4 ds, cl, repeat from * across. Tie and cut. **8th row:** R 4 ds, 2 p sep by 2 ds, 2 ds, j to center p of first r (last row), *2 ds, 2 p sep by 2 ds, 4 ds, cl, sp (¼-inch), turn, sr 3 ds, lp, 3 ds, cl, turn, sp, r 4 ds, j to fifth p of opposite r, 2 ds, p, 2 ds, j in center p of next r (last row), 2 ds, 2 p sep by 2 ds, 4 ds, cl, turn, sp, sr 3 ds, j to lp of last sr, 3 ds, cl, turn, sp, r 4 ds, j to fifth p of opposite r, 2 ds, p, 2 ds, j to center p of next r (last row), repeat from * across. Tie and cut. **9th row:** R 4 ds, 5 p sep by 2 ds, 4 ds, cl, *turn, sp, 3 ds, j in lp of sr (last row), 3 ds, cl, turn, sp, r 4 ds, j to fifth p of r, 2 ds, 4 p sep by 2 ds, 4 ds, cl, turn, sp, sr 3 ds, j in same lp with last sr, 3 ds, cl, turn, sp, r 4 ds, j to fifth p of r, 2 ds, 4 p sep by 2 ds, 4 ds, cl, repeat from * across. Tie and cut. **10th row:** Repeat seventh row. **11th row:** Repeat fourth row, sk 1 r (last row) between center p of the 2 ch. **12th row:** Repeat fifth row. **13th row:** Repeat eighth row around the entire cap. Tie and cut.

THE LOWER CAP

(Two Shuttles)

For Crown: Center Medallion: R 8 lp sep by 3 ds, cl, tie and cut, *sr 3 ds, j to lp of center r, 3 ds, cl, ch 4 ds, 3 p sep by 3 ds, 4 ds. Repeat from * around, j to sr, tie and cut. *Sr 3 ds, j to first p on ch, 3 ds, cl, ch 6 ds, 3 p sep by 3 ds, 6 ds, sr 3 ds, sk 1 p on same ch, j in next p, 3 ds, cl, ch 6 ds, 3 p sep by 3 ds, 6 ds, sr 3 ds, j in center p of next ch, 3 ds, cl, ch 6 ds, 3 p sep by 3 ds, 6 ds. Repeat from * around, tie and cut. Make nine small motifs, using only first row around center r, j each motif to center p of each ch, on large motif j each small motif together by center p on ch, leaving 33 p-ch free around motif.
1st row around: Sr 3 ds, j to a center p on ch, 3 ds, cl, *ch 6 ds, 5 p sep by 3 ds, 6 ds, sr 3 ds, j to center p of next p-ch, 3 ds, cl. Repeat from * around, tie and cut. **2d row:** Sr 3 ds, 3 lp sep by 2 ds, 3 ds, cl, turn, *ch 12 ds, sr 3 ds, p, 2 ds, j to second p of ch in last row, 2 ds, p, 3 ds, cl, turn, *ch 12 ds, sr 3 ds, j to third lp of sr, 2 ds, 2 lp sep by 2 ds, 3 ds, cl, turn, ch 12 ds, sr 3 ds, j to third p of r, 2 ds, sk 1 p on ch, j to next p, 2 ds, p, 3 ds, cl, turn,

(Continued on page 15)

Baby Bonnet

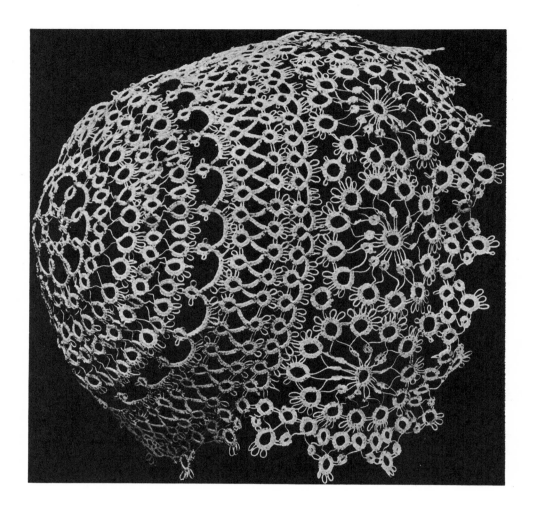

Crochet Cotton No. 50.

CENTER FIGURE—8 r of 3 p, sep by 3 ds, leaving short sp between, tie and cut.

1st Row—R 6 ds, j to p of center figure, 6 ds, cl—ch 3 p, sep by 3 ds—rep around center figure, tie and cut.

2d Row—With only shuttle thread, sr, 3 p, sep by 4 ds; j center p to 1st p of ch, last row—sp ¾ inch—turn—lr 5 ds, 7 p, sep by 2 ds, 5 ds, cl—sp as before—turn—rep 2nd r, j all sr to p of ch and to each other and j lr to each other by 1st p—tie and cut.

3d Row—Rep 2nd row, j sr to 3rd and 5th p of lr, last row and making lr with only 5 p—tie and cut. The next 3 rows use 2 threads.

4th Row—R, 3 p, sep by 3 ds, j center p to center p of lr, last ro —ch 3 ds, 7 p, sep by 1 ds, 3 ds—rep around, j r to every third lr of last row, tie and cut.

5th Row—R, 3 ds, 5 p, sep by 2 ds, 3 ds, cl—turn—ch 5 ds—rep r, j center p to 2nd p of ch, last row—rep ch—rep from beginning of row, j r of outer edge by 1st p and j inner r to 2nd and 6th p of ch, (last row.)

6th Row—R, 4 ds, 5 p, sep by 2 ds, j center p to center p of r, last row,) cl—ch 3 p, sep by 2 ds—rep around until there are 37 ch, j first medallion to 2nd ch.

Make 7 medallions as follows—

CENTER RING—12 p, sep by 1 ds, cl—tie and cut.

1st Row—With only one thread—Sr, 3 ds, j to p of center r, 3 ds, cl—sp (¾ inch)—turn—lr, 6 ds, 7 p, sep by 1 ds, 6 ds, cl—sp as before—rep from beginning of 1st row, j sr to p of center r and j lr to each other by 1st p; j two lr to cap by center p to center p of 2nd, and 3rd ch. (6th row.)

J each new medallion to preceding one by 2 r leaving 1 r free between this and j of cap, leaving also 3 ch free on cap. Fill in space thus left by r, 2 ds, 5 p, sep by 3 ds, 1 ds, cl—j 1st, 3rd and 5th p to center p of free r and center ch—tie and cut. Fill space at outer edge with r of 1 ds, 8 p, sep by 3 ds, 2 ds, j as before, cl—tie and cut.

EDGE OF CAP—Beginning at end of 6th row—R 3 p, sep by 3 ds, j center p to free p of 1st r, 6th row, cl—sp not more than ¼ inch—turn—Sr, 3 ds, p, 3 ds, cl—sp as before—turn—rep 1st r, this row) j 1st p to 1st r and center p to 1st p of ch, 6th row—sp—turn—lr, 3 ds, j to p of sr, 3 ds, 3 p, sep by 2 ds, 3 ds, p, 3 ds, cl—sp—rep 1st r, j 1st p as before to corresponding preceding r—sp—turn—rep sr, j to last p of lr.

Kep edge around, j where possible to keep work smooth.

Baby Socklet and Shoe

Crochet Cotton No. 30.

1st Row—Sr, 3 ds, p, 3 ds, cl,—sp (⅜ inch)—turn—lr, 3 p, sep by 3 ds, cl—sp—turn—rep sr, j to p of last sr—sp—turn—rep lr, j to p of last lr—rep to desired length.

Rep 1st row, j 2 sr to corresponding group, last **row**, this forms a beading.

Rose—R, 5 ds, p, 5 ds, cl—ch 5 p, sep by 2 ds—rep from beginning 4 times, j all r to p of 1st r—tie and cut.

View of Shoe (Top and Sole)

Crochet Cotton No. 30.

Sole of Shoe—Composed of 2 rows, made with shuttle only.

1st Row—Beginning at heel, make 1 clover leaf of 3 r of 3 p, sep by 5 ds, j each to other as in all clover leaves—turn—sp not more than ¼ inch—sr, 4 ds, p, 4 ds, cl—turn—sp as before—lr, 3 ds, j to last p of clover leaf, 3 ds, p, 2 ds, p, 3 ds, p, 3 ds, cl—turn—sp—rep sr, j to p of last sr—turn—sp—rep lr, j to last p of preceding lr—rep from first sr; j, sr in groups of two—rep until there are 6 groups of sr and 11 lr. Going from last sr, rep clover leaf, j 1st p to p of preceding lr—rep along this side, j sr to opposite groups, making 4 in each group and j lr, before last sr to last p of clover leaf. After last sr, tie to end left at clover leaf, cut.

Outer Row of Sole—R 3 ds, p, 2 ds, j to 1st p of lr (preceding clover leaf), 2 ds, j to next p, 3 ds, p; 3 ds, cl—turn—ch 3 ds, p, 2 ds, p, 3 ds—rep r, and ch around, j to all p and j to same p where clover leaf is j—Around clover leaf adding 1 ds on each side of j and making r of only 3 p where there is only 1 p to j Rep, outer row, this time making all r the same as 1st r.

Make Medallion No. 30* and sew in place on one end for toe, fill in corners at top of shoe with one scallop of edge of medallion. Beginning at j of medallion, rep 1st and 2nd rows made, to make a beading around top. This is like the center of sole, except on last row at top make ch instead of r, tie and cut.

*See page 20

Rectangular Doily

(Two Shuttles)

The attractive lacy table set, shown on page 3, may be made of either SILKINE CROCHET COTTON or STAR CROCHET COTTON in size 50, and 10 balls are needed for 7 pieces. May be made also of size 30.

Make 2 medallions for center as follows: R 3 ds, 12 p sep by 3 ds, 3 ds, cl, tie and cut.

1st row: Lr 4 ds, 9 p sep by 3 ds, 4 ds, cl, *turn, sp (3-16-inch) sr 5 ds, j to p of center r, 5 ds, cl, turn, sp, lr, 4 ds, j to ninth p of last lr, 3 ds, 8 p sep by 3 ds, 4 ds, cl, repeat from * around. Tie and cut.

2d row: Lr 4 ds, 9 p sep by 3 ds, 4 ds, cl, *turn, sp, sr 5 ds, j to fourth p of lr (last row), 5 ds, cl, turn, sp, lr 4 ds, p, 3 ds, j to eighth p of last lr, 3 ds, 7 p sep by 3 ds, 4 ds, cl, turn, sp, sr 5 ds, sk 1 p of same lr (last row), j in next p, 5 ds, cl, turn, sp, lr 4 ds, p, 3 ds, j to eighth p of last lr, 3 ds, 7 p sep by 3 ds, 4 ds, cl, repeat from * around. Tie and cut.

Join the 2 medallions together by center p of 3 lr, make 2 small motifs between the 2 medallions as follows: (R 4 ds, 4 p sep by 4 ds, 4 ds, j to center p of the third r from where the medallions are joined, 4 ds, 4 p sep by 4 ds, 4 ds, cl) 2 times, r 4 ds, 9 p sep by 4 ds, 4 ds, cl. Tie and cut.

Make 4 motifs same as other 2 motifs for corner, sk 4 r from other motif, j to center p of next r, sk 1 r and j to next r.

Make an insertion to go across the ends of the center as follows: R 5 ds, 9 p sep by 4 ds, 5 ds, cl, turn, ch 20 ds, turn, r 5 ds, 9 p sep by 4 ds, 5 ds, cl, (turn, ch 20 ds, turn, r 5 ds, p, 4 ds, j to eighth p of opposite r, 4 ds, 7 p sep by 4 ds, 5 ds, cl) 5 times, (turn, ch 20 ds, r 5 ds, p, 4 ds, j to eighth p of opposite r, 4 ds, 2 p sep by 4 ds, 4 ds, j to center p of first lr on medallion to right of small motif, 4 ds, 4 p sep by 4 ds, 5 ds, cl, turn, ch 20 ds, turn, r 5 ds, p, 4 ds, j to eighth p of opposite r, 4 ds, 7 p sep by 4 ds, 5 ds, cl) 3 times, (turn, ch 20 ds, turn, r 5 ds, p, 4 ds, j to eighth p of opposite r, 4 ds, 7 p sep by 4 ds, 5 ds., cl) 6 times. Tie and cut.

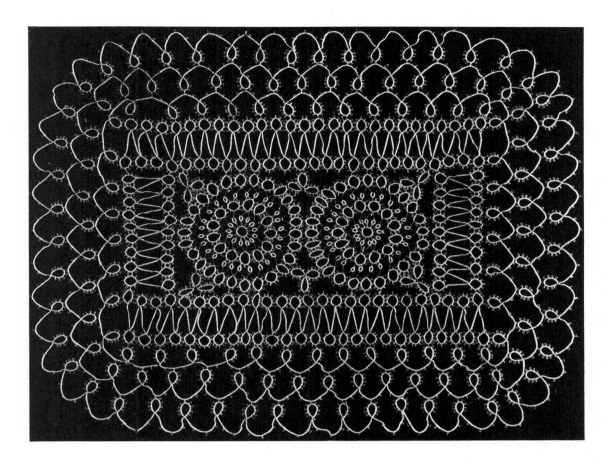

Make the sides in the same way, allowing 4 r across side of insertion, j center p of first r to second p on side of first r at end and center p of fourth r to second p of next r, and j center p of r of small motif to seventh p of the same r, 3 rings between the 3 rings that j to the large medallion, then make 3 rings, j the center p of third r to center p of r of motif.

This is half-way across 1 side. Reverse directions for the other half. Tie and cut. Work the other side in same way.

For Lacy Edge: R 5 ds, 4 p sep by 4 ds, 4 ds, j in center p of corner r, 4 ds, 4 p sep by 4 ds, 5 ds, cl, turn, ch 8 ds, 3 p sep by 8 ds, 8 ds, turn, r 5 ds, 4 p sep by 4 ds, 4 ds, sk 2 p of same r at corner, j to next p, 4 ds, 4 p sep by 4 ds, 5 ds, cl, turn, ch 8 ds, 3 p sep by 8 ds, 8 ds, turn, r 5 ds, 4 p sep by 4 ds, 4 ds, j in second p of next r on end of doily, 4 ds, 4 p sep by 4 ds, 5 ds, cl, turn, ch 8 ds, 3 p sep by 8 ds, 8 ds, turn, repeat the r and ch, sk 1 r of last row, j next r in center p of next r (last row) around, j 2 r to each corner r. Tie and cut.

Next 2 rows: Make same as first row, j r to center p of each ch, at corners j r to first and third p. Tie and cut.

BABY CAPS

(Continued from page 11)

ch 12 ds, sr 3 ds, j to third p of r, 2 ds, 2 p sep by 2 ds, 3 ds, cl, turn, ch 12 ds, sr 3 ds, j to third p of r, 2 ds, j to second p of next ch, 2 ds, p, 3 ds, cl, turn, repeat from * 14 times, (then add an extra r between 2 ch loops of last row at intervals until there are 13 extra r. This part is at bottom and sides of cap. **3d row:** R 3 ds, p, 2 ds, j to a p of r (last row), 2 ds, p, 3 ds, cl, *ch 6 ds, 3 p sep by 2 ds, 6 ds, r 3 ds, p, 3 ds, sk 1 r of last row, j to p of next r, 2 ds, p, 3 ds, cl, repeat around until there are 34 ch. **4th row:** *R 4 ds, 3 p sep by 3 ds, 4 ds, cl, turn, sp (½-inch), r 4 ds, p, 3 ds, j to center p of ch (last row), 3 ds, p, 4 ds, cl, turn, sp, r 4 ds, j to p of r, 3 ds, 2 p sep by 3 ds, 4 ds, cl, turn, sp, r 4 ds, j to p of r 3 ds, 2 p sep by 3 ds, 4 ds, cl, turn, sp. Repeat from *, j each r together, and every other r to p of ch (last row). **5th row:** R 4 ds, 3 p sep by 2 ds, 4 ds, cl, *lr 5 ds, j to third p of r, 6 p sep by 2 ds, 5 ds, cl, r 4 ds, j to last p of lr, 2 ds, 2 p sep by 2 ds, 4 ds, cl, ch 7 ds, p, 2 ds, j to p of third r (last row), 2 ds, p, 7 ds, r 4 ds, p, 2 ds, j to center p of last r, 2 ds, p, 4 ds, cl, sk 1 r (last row), j to p of next r, 2 ds, 2 p sep by 2 ds, 4 ds, cl, ch 6 ds, r 4 ds, p, 2 ds, j to fifth p of lr, 2 ds, p, 4 ds, cl, r 4 ds, 3 p sep by 2 ds, 4 ds, cl, ch 8 ds, lr 5 ds, j to center p of last sr, 2 ds, 6 p sep by 2 ds, 5 ds, cl, ch 8 ds, sr 4 ds, p, 2 ds, j to last p of lr, 2 ds, p, 4 ds, cl, sr 4 ds, 3 p sep by 2 ds, 4 ds, cl, ch 6 ds, sr 4 ds, p, 2 ds, j to center p of opposite sr, 2 ds, j to p of next r (last row), 4 ds, cl, r 4 ds, 3 p sep by 2 ds, 4 ds, cl, ch 6 ds, p, 2 ds, sk 1 sr of last row, j to p of next r, 2 ds, p, 2 ds, j to center p of opposite r, 2 ds, p, 4 ds, cl. Repeat from * across, tie and cut. **6th row:** Make like fifth row, only j to center p of lr on the points together. **7th row:** R 4 ds, 2 p sep by 2 ds, 2 ds, j to center p of ch (last row), 2 ds, 2 p sep by 2 ds, 4 ds, cl, sp (¼-inch), turn, *sr 3 ds, lp, 3 ds, cl, turn, sp, r 4 ds, j to fifth p of r, 2 ds, p, 2 ds, j to center p of next ch (last row), 2 ds, 2 p sep by 2 ds, 4 ds, cl, turn, sp, r 3 ds, j in lp of sr, 3 ds, cl, turn, sp, r 4 ds, j to last p of r, 2 ds, p, 2 ds, j to center p of r (last row), 2 ds, 2 p sep by 2 ds, 4 ds, cl. Repeat from *, j r to sr and center p of ch of last row, tie and cut. **8th row:** Made like seventh row, only j two sr in lp. **9th row:** R 4 ds, 2 p sep by 2 ds, 2 ds, *j to center p of r (last row), 2 ds, 2 p sep by 2 ds, 4 ds, cl, turn, sp (¼-inch), sr 3 ds, p, 3 ds, cl, turn, sp, r 4 ds, j to last p of r, 2 ds, p, 2 ds, j to center p of r (last row), 2 ds, 2 p sep by 2 ds, 4 ds, cl, turn, sp, r 4 ds, j to p of sr, 2 ds, 4 p sep by 2 ds, 5 ds, cl, turn, sp, 4 ds, j to p of r, 2 ds, p, 2 ds, j to center p of r (last row), 2 ds, 2 p sep by 2 ds, 4 ds, cl, turn, sp, r 3 ds, j to last p of lr, 3 ds, cl, turn, sp, r 4 ds, j to p of r, 2 ds, p, 2 ds. Repeat from * around edge of cap.

15

Medallions

SQUARE MEDALLION No. 1
(Two Shuttles)

R 5 ds, 5 p sep by 3 ds, 5 ds, cl, (r 5 ds, j to fifth p of last r, 3 ds, 4 p sep by 3 ds, 5 ds, cl) 3 times, j last r to first r. Tie and cut. Make 3 more motifs like first one, j together by the 2 p on each side. Form a square of the 4 motifs. **Edge:** *R 8 ds, j to second p to right from center side of the 2 motifs, 3 ds, p, 3 ds, sk 1 p on next r, j in next p, 8 ds, cl, turn, ch 4 ds, 5 p sep by 2 ds, 4 ds, r 8 ds, j in second p of corner r, 3 ds, 2 p sep by 3 ds, 8 ds, cl, ch 4 ds, 7 p sep by 2 ds, 4 ds, r 8 ds, j to third p of last r, 3 ds, p, 3 ds, sk 1 p on corner r, j in next p, 8 ds, cl, ch 4 ds, 5 p sep by 2 ds, 4 ds, repeat from * around. Tie and cut.

SQUARE MEDALLION No. 2
(Two Shuttles)

R 9 ds, 5 p sep by 3 ds, 9 ds, cl, (r 9 ds, j to fifth p of last r, 3 ds, 4 p sep by 3 ds, 9 ds, cl) twice, l ch 10 ds, p, 10 ds, *(r 9 ds, j to fifth p of last r, 3 ds, 4 p sep by 3 ds, 9 ds, cl) 3 times, l ch 10 ds, j in p of l ch, 10 ds. Repeat from * two more times. Join to first group of rings. Tie and cut. **Edge:** *R 3 ds, p, 3 ds, j in fourth p of r to right of center corner ring, 3 ds, p, 3 ds, cl, ch 8 ds, 3 p sep by 2 ds, 8 ds, r 3 ds, 3 p sep by 3 ds, 3 ds, cl, lr 3 ds, j to third p of last r, 3 ds, p, 3 ds, j to center p of next lr, 3 ds, 2 p sep by 3 ds, 3 ds, cl, r 3 ds, j to last p of lr, 3 ds, 2 p sep by 3 ds, 3 ds, cl, ch 8 ds, 3 p sep by 2 ds, 8 ds, r 3 ds, p, 3 ds, j in second p of next r, 3 ds, p, 3 ds, cl, ch 8 ds, 3 p sep by 2 ds, 8 ds, repeat from * around. J in first r. Tie and cut.

LARGE ROUND POINTED MEDALLION No. 3
(Two Shuttles)

For center: R 10 ds, p, 10 ds, cl, ch 1 ds, 9 p sep by 2 ds, j in p of r, 9 p sep by 2 ds. Tie and cut. **1st row:** R 5 ds, p, 4 ds, j to a p of center, 4 ds, p, 5 ds, cl, *ch 5 ds, 3 p sep by 3 ds, 5 ds, r 5 ds, p, 4 ds, sk 1 p, j in next p, 4 ds, p, 5 ds, cl, repeat from * around. Tie and cut. **2d Row:** R 4 ds, p, 4 ds, j to center p of ch (last row), 4 ds, p, 4 ds, cl, turn, (ch 8 ds, r 4 ds, 3 p sep by 4 ds, 4 ds, cl) 3 times, ch 8 ds, loop thread around first ch-8 ds, *ch 15 ds, r 4 ds, p, 4 ds, j to center p of next ch (last row), 4 ds, p, 4 ds, cl, ch 8 ds, r 4 ds, p, 4 ds, j in center p of opposite r, 4 ds, p, 4 ds, cl, (ch 8 ds, r 4 ds, 3 p sep by 4 ds, 4 ds, cl) twice, ch 8 ds, sl st around first ch-8 ds, repeat from * around. Tie and cut.

ROUND MEDALLION No. 4
(Two Shuttles)

Center ring: 16 lp, cl, tie and cut. **1st row:** Sr 4 ds, j in lp of center r, 4 ds, cl, turn, ch 12 ds, lr 8 ds, 5 p sep by 3 ds, 8 ds, cl, *turn, ch 12 ds, sr 4 ds, j to next p on center ring, 4 ds, cl, turn, ch 12 ds, lr 8 ds, j to fifth p of last lr, 3 ds, 4 p sep by 3 ds, 8 ds, cl, repeat from * around. Tie and cut.

MEDALLION No. 5
(Two Shuttles)

1st row: *R 3 ds, 3 p sep by 3 ds, 3 ds, cl, sp (⅛-inch), repeat from * 5 times, j each r to other by first and last p—(6 rings in all). Tie and cut. **2d row:** *R 3 ds, j to p of first row, 3 ds, p, 3 ds, cl, ch 3 ds, 5 p sep by 2 ds, 3 ds, repeat from * around. Tie and cut. **3d row:** *R 3 ds, 3 p sep by 3 ds, 4 ds, cl, lr 3 ds j to third p of last r, 3 ds, p, 3 ds, j to center p of ch of last row, 3 ds, p, 3 ds, p, 4 ds, cl, r 4 ds, j to last p of lr, 3 ds, 2 p sep by 3 ds, 3 ds, cl, ch 4 ds, 8 p sep by 2 ds, 4 ds, r 4 ds, p, 3 ds, j to second p of next ch, 3 ds, p, 4 ds, cl, ch 4 ds, p, 4 ds, j in last p of last ring, 3 ds, sk 1 p on ch, j in next p on ch, 3 ds, p, 4 ds, cl, ch 4 ds, 8 p sep by 2 ds, 4 ds, repeat from * around. Tie and cut.

SMALL SQUARE MEDALLION No. 6
(Two Shuttles)

Make 4 small motifs for center:—R 8 ds, lp, 8 ds, cl, (ch 5 ds, p, 5 ds, p, 5 ds, r 8 ds, j to lp, 8 ds, cl) 3 times, ch 5 ds, p, 5 ds, p, 5 ds, j to first ch. Tie and cut. Make 3 motifs like first one, join first to second by the 2 p on side. Join next 2 motifs, so they form a square. *R 8 ds, j to p on ch, 8 ds, cl, ch 8 ds, 3 p sep by 3 ds, 8 ds, repeat from * around.

SMALL TATTED MEDALLION No. 7
(Two Shuttles)

Center ring: 8 lp with 2 ds between, cl, tie and cut. **1st row:** *Sr 3 ds, j to lp of center r, 3 ds, cl, ch 5 ds, 3 p sep by 2 ds, 5 ds, repeat from * around, tie and cut. **2d row:** *Sr 3 ds, j in center p of ch (last row), 3 ds, cl, ch 6 ds, 3 p sep by 2 ds, 6 ds, sr 3 ds, j in first p of next ch, 3 ds, cl, ch 6 ds, 3 p sep by 2 ds, 6 ds, sr 3 ds, sk 1 p on same ch, j in next p, 3 ds, cl, ch 6 ds, 3 p sep by 2 ds, 6 ds, repeat from * around. Tie and cut.

SMALL ROUND TATTED MEDALLION No. 8
(Two Shuttles)

1st row: R 4 ds, 3 p sep by 4 ds, 4 ds, cl, sp (⅛-inch) (r 4 ds, j to third p of last r, 4 ds, 3 p sep by 4 ds, 4 ds, cl) j the last p of sixth r to first p of first r. Tie and cut. **2d row:** *(Sr 4 ds, 3 p sep by 4 ds, 4 ds, cl) 2 times, ch 10 ds, sr 4 ds, 3 p sep by 4 ds, 4 ds, cl, turn work. Lr, 7 ds, j to third p of opposite sr, 3 ds, j to p of center motif, 3 ds, p, 7 ds, cl, ch 10 ds, repeat from * around. Tie and cut.

SQUARE MEDALLION No. 9
(Two Shuttles)

(R 3 ds, 3 p sep by 3 ds, 3 ds, cl, lr 4 ds, j to third p of last r, 3 ds, p, 3 ds, lp, 3 ds, 2 p sep by 3 ds, 4 ds, cl, r 3 ds, j to last p of lr, 3 ds, 2 p sep by 3 ds, 3 ds, cl, turn, ch 6 ds, 5 p sep by 3 ds, 6 ds), 4 times. Join center p of lr in lp of first lr. Tie and cut. **Next row:** *R 4 ds, p, 3 ds, j to first p at right of ch (last row), 3 ds, p, 4 ds, cl, turn, ch 6 ds, 3 p sep by 2 ds, 6 ds, r 4 ds, j to third p of last r, 3 ds, j in next p on ch, 3 ds, p, 4 ds, cl, turn, ch 6 ds, 3 p sep by 2 ds, 6 ds, turn, r 3 ds, 3 p sep by 3 ds, 3 ds, cl, lr 4 ds, j to third p of last r, 3 ds, j to p of opposite r, 3 ds, j in next p of ch, 3 ds, 2 p sep by 3 ds, 4 ds, cl, sr 3 ds, j in last p of lr, 3 ds, 2 p sep by 3 ds, 3 ds, cl, ch 6 ds, 3 p sep by 2 ds, 6 ds, r 4 ds, j to p of ch, 3 ds, j to next p on ch, 3 ds, p, 4 ds, cl, ch 6 ds, 3 p sep by 2 ds, 6 ds, r 4 ds, j to p of opposite r, 3 ds, j to next p on ch, 3 ds, p, 4 ds, cl, ch 6 ds, 3 p sep by 2 ds, 6 ds, repeat from * around.

ROUND MEDALLION No. 10
(One Shuttle)

Center motif: (Lr 10 ds, 7 p sep by 3 ds, 10 ds, cl) 5 times, j first p of each r to seventh p of last r and seventh p to first p for last r. Tie and cut. *Sr 4 ds, p, 3 ds, j to second free p of lr, 3 ds, p, 4 ds, cl, turn, sp, (¼-inch) r 8 ds, p, 4 ds, 3 p sep by 2 ds, 4 ds, p, 8 ds, cl, turn, sp, sr 4 ds, j to third p of last sr, 3 ds, j to next p on lr, 3 ds, p, 4 ds, cl, **turn, sp, r 8 ds, j to fifth p of last r, 4 ds, 3 p sep by 2 ds, 4 ds, p, 8 ds, cl, turn, sp, sr 4 ds, j to third p of last sr, 3 ds, j to next p on same lr, 3 ds, p, 4 ds, cl, turn, sp, repeat from **around. Do not j next sr to center motif—j next 2 sr to third and fifth ps of next lr of center motif, then repeat from * around. Tie and cut.

ROUND MEDALLION No. 11
(Two Shuttles)

Center ring: 8 lp, cl. **1st row:** *R 4 ds, j to lp of center r, 4 ds, cl, ch 4 ds, 3 p sep by 2 ds, 4 ds, repeat from * around, tie and cut. **2d row:** *Sr 3 ds, 3 p sep by 3 ds, 3 ds, cl, lr

(Continued on page 30)

Medallions

MEDALLION No. 16

(Two Shuttles)

Center: (Sr 4 ds, p, 4 ds, cl, lr 4 ds, j to p of sr, 4 ds, lp, 4 ds, p, 4 ds, cl, sr 4 ds, j to third p of lr, 4 ds, cl, turn, ch 6 ds, 2 p sep by 5 ds, 6 ds, turn) 4 times, j each lr to lp of first lr. Tie and cut. **Edge:** *Sr 4 ds, p, 4 ds, cl, lr 4 ds, j to p of sr, 4 ds, 2 p sep by 4 ds, 4 ds, cl, sr 4 ds, j to third p of lr, 4 ds, cl, turn, ch 9 ds, turn, r 4 ds, j to first p of ch of center, 4 ds, cl, turn, ch 9 ds, turn, sr 4 ds, j to p of opposite sr, 4 ds, cl, lr 4 ds, j to same p with sr, 4 ds, 2 p sep by 4 ds, 4 ds, cl, sr 4 ds, j to third p of lr, 4 ds, cl, turn, ch 9 ds, turn, sr 4 ds, j in same p with last sr on ch, turn, ch 9 ds, turn. Repeat from * around, placing 3 sr in next p of ch, continue around, alternating 2 sr and 3 sr in the picots of chains.

POINTED MEDALLION No. 17

(Two Shuttles)

Center motif: R 4 ds, 3 p sep by 4 ds, 4 ds, cl, *turn, ch 6 ds, 5 p sep by 2 ds, 6 ds, turn, r 4 ds, j in third p of last r, 4 ds, 2 p sep by 4 ds, 4 ds, cl. Repeat from * around. Tie and cut. **Next row:** R 3 ds, 2 p sep by 3 ds, 3 ds, j in second p of ch (center motif), 3 ds, cl, r 3 ds, sk 1 p on same ch, j in next p, 3 ds, 2 p sep by 3 ds, 3 ds, cl, turn, ch 9 ds, (r 3 ds, 3 p sep by 3 ds, 3 ds, cl) 2 times, ch 9 ds, turn, *r 2 ds, 3 p sep by 2 ds, 2 ds, cl, (r 2 ds, j to third p of last r, 2 ds 2 p sep by 2 ds, 2 ds, cl) 2 times, turn, ch 9 ds, r 3 ds, p, 3 ds, j in center p of opposite r, 3 ds, p, 3 ds, cl, r 3 ds, 3 p sep by 3 ds, 3 ds, cl, ch 9 ds, turn, r 3 ds, p, 3 ds, j in center p of opposite r, 3 ds, p, 3 ds, cl, r 3 ds, 3 p sep by 3 ds, 3 ds, cl, turn, ch 9 ds, r 3 ds, p, 3 ds, j in center p of opposite r, 3 ds, p, 3 ds, cl, r 3 ds, 3 p sep by 3 ds, 3 ds, cl, ch 9 ds, turn, r 2 ds, 3 p sep by 2 ds, 2 ds, cl, (r 2 ds, j to third p of last r, 2 ds, 2 p sep by 2 ds, 2 ds, cl) 2 times, turn, ch 9 ds, r 3 ds, p, 3 ds, j in center p of opposite r, 3 ds, p, 3 ds, cl, r 3 ds, 3 p sep by 3 ds, 3 ds, cl, ch 9 ds, turn, r 3 ds, p, 3 ds, j to center p of opposite r, 3 ds, j in second p of next ch, 3 ds, cl, r 3 ds, sk 1 p of same ch, j in next p, 3 ds, 2 p sep by 3 ds, 3 ds, cl, turn, ch 9 ds, r 3 ds, p, 3 ds, j in center p of opposite r, 3 ds, p, 3 ds, cl, r 3 ds, 3 p sep by 3 ds, 3 ds, cl. Repeat from * around. Tie and cut.

ROUND TATTED MEDALLION No. 18

(Two Shuttles)

Center: R 16 p, cl, tie and cut. **1st row:** Sr 4 ds, j to p on center r, 4 ds, cl, turn, sp (¼-inch), lr 5 ds, 5 p sep by 3 ds, 5 ds, cl, *turn, sp, sr 4 ds, j to next p on center r, 4 ds, cl, turn, sp, lr, 5 ds, j in fifth p of last lr, 3 ds, 4 p sep by 3 ds, 5 ds, cl, repeat from * around. Tie and cut. **2d row:** *R 4 ds, j to center p of lr (last row), 4 ds, cl, turn, ch 8 ds, 3 p sep by 2 ds, 8 ds, turn, repeat from * around. Tie and cut.

POINTED MEDALLION No. 19

(Two Shuttles)

Center r, 8 lp sep by 2 ds, cl. Tie and cut. **1st row:** *Sr 5 ds, j in lp of center r, 5 ds, cl, turn, ch 7 ds, p, 7 ds, turn, repeat from * around. Tie and cut. **2d row:** Sr 5 ds, j to p of ch (last row), 5 ds, cl, *turn, (ch 4 ds, sr 3 ds, p, 3 ds, cl) 2 times, ch 4 ds, turn, lr 4 ds, 3 p sep by 4 ds, 4 ds, cl, (r 4 ds, j in third p of last r, 4 ds, 2 p sep by 4 ds, 4 ds, cl) 2 times, turn, (ch 4 ds, sr 3 ds, p, 3 ds, cl) 2 times, 4 ds, turn, r 5 ds, j to p of next ch, 5 ds, cl, **repeat** from * around. Tie and cut.

MEDALLION No. 20

(Two Shuttles)

Center motif: R 8 ds, p, 8 ds, cl, ch 2 ds, 9 p sep by 2 ds, j in p of r, 9 ds sep by 2 ds. Tie and cut. **1st row:** R 5 ds, j in a p of motif, 5 ds, cl, *turn, ch 4 ds, 3 p sep by 2 ds, 4 ds, turn, r 5 ds, sk 1 p of motif, j in next p, 5 ds, cl. Repeat from * around. Tie and cut. **2d row:** *R 3 ds, p, 2 ds, j in center p of ch (last row), 2 ds, p, 3 ds, cl, turn, ch 4 ds, 3 p sep by 2 ds, 4 ds, turn, r 3 ds, p, 2 ds, j in same p with last r, 2 ds, p, 3 ds, cl, turn, ch 4 ds, 3 p sep by 2 ds, 4 ds, turn. Repeat from * around. Tie and cut.

POINTED TATTED MEDALLION No. 21

(Two Shuttles)

Center motif: R 3 ds, 5 p sep by 3 ds, 3 ds, cl, (turn, ch 7 ds, 3 p sep by 2 ds, 7 ds, turn, r 3 ds, p, 3 ds, j in fourth p of last r, 3 ds, 3 p sep by 3 ds, 3 ds, cl) 7 times, turn, ch 7 ds, 3 p sep by 2 ds, 7 ds. Tie and cut. **Next row:** R 9 p, cl, ch 6 ds, p, 2 ds, j third p of ch, 2 ds, p, 6 ds, p, 6 ds, turn, r 4 p, j in center p of last r, 4 p, cl, *turn (ch 7 ds, turn, r, 9 p, cl) twice, turn, ch 6 ds, j in p of opposite ch, 6 ds, p, 2 ds, j in first p of next ch (center motif), 2 ds, p, 6 ds, turn, r 4 p, j in center p of last r, 4 p, cl, turn, ch 6 ds, p, 2 ds, sk 1 p, j in next p of same ch (center motif), 2 ds, p, 6 ds, p, 6 ds, turn, r 4 p, j in p with last r, 4 p, cl, repeat from * around. Tie and cut.

SMALL MEDALLION No. 22

(Two Shuttles)

R 9 ds, 6 p sep by 3 ds, 9 ds, cl, (r 9 ds, j to sixth p of last r, 3 ds, 5 p sep by 3 ds, 9 ds, cl) 3 times, j last r to first r by first and last p. Tie and cut. R 5 ds, j in a p of center motif, 5 ds, cl, *turn, ch 6 ds, 3 p sep by 2 ds, 6 ds, turn, r 5 ds, j to next p on motif, 5 ds, cl, repeat from * around, j in first r. Tie and cut.

MEDALLION No. 23

(Two Shuttles)

Center: R 8 p sep by 2 ds, cl, tie and cut. **1st row:** Lr 5 ds, 5 p sep by 5 ds, 5 ds, cl, *turn, ch 3 ds, j to p of center ring, 3 ds, turn, sr 5 ds, j to fifth p of last r, 5 ds, 2 p sep by 5 ds, 5 ds, cl, turn, ch 3 ds, j to next p of center r, 3 ds, turn, lr, 5 ds, j to third p of last r, 5 ds, 4 p sep by 5 ds, 5 ds, cl, repeat from * around, j to first r. Tie and cut. **2d row:** *Sr 6 ds, j to center p of sr (last row), 6 ds, cl, turn, ch 7 ds, p, 7 ds, turn, sr 6 ds, j to first p on lr, 6 ds, cl, turn, ch 7 ds, p, 7 ds, turn, sr 6 ds, sk 1 p of lr, j in next p, 6 ds, cl, turn, ch 7 ds, p, 7 ds, turn, repeat from * around, j. Tie and cut.

ROUND MEDALLION No. 24

(Two Shuttles)

R 3 ds, 5 p sep by 3 ds, 3 ds, cl, (turn, ch 3 ds, 5 p sep by 3 ds, 3 ds, turn, r 3 ds, p, 3 ds, j in fourth p of last r, 3 ds, 3 p sep by 3 ds, 3 ds, cl) 5 times, turn, ch 3 ds, 5 p sep by 3 ds, 3 ds, j in first r with first ch. Tie and cut. R 3 ds, 5 p sep by 3 ds, 3 ds, cl, *r 3 ds, j in fifth p of last r, 3 ds, 3 p sep by 3 ds, 3 ds, j in center p of ch (last row), 3 ds, 2 p sep by 3 ds, 3 ds, cl, r 3 ds, j to fifth p of last r, 3 ds, 4 p sep by 3 ds, 3 ds, cl, turn, ch 8 ds, 5 p sep by 3 ds, 8 ds, turn, sr 3 ds, j in center p of last r, 3 ds, 2 p sep by 3 ds, 3 ds, cl, turn, ch 8 ds, 5 p sep by 3 ds, 8 ds, turn, r 3 ds, 2 p sep by 3 ds, 3 ds, j in third p of sr, 3 ds, 2 p sep by 3 ds, 3 ds, cl, repeat from * around. Tie and cut.

(Continued on page 31)

Medallions

Rose Medallion No. 30 to Match Edging No. 39 (p. 27)
Crochet Cotton No. 40.

ROSE CENTER—Use directions of Plate 39 for 3 rows of rose; last row of rose, as follows: Ch 3 ds, 4 p, sep by 2 ds, 3 ds, tie and cut.

EDGE—R 6 ds, p, 6 ds, cl—ch 3 ds, 4 p, sep by 2 ds, 3 ds—rep r 3 times, sep by same ch, j all r to p of 1st r—ch 3 ds, j to 2nd p of ch of rose, 2 ds, j to next p, 3 ds—rep edge around, j 2nd p of 1st new ch to opposite p of preceding ch, tie and cut.

Medallion No. 31

Crochet Cotton No. 40.

CENTER FIGURE—6 r, of 3 p, sep by 5 ds, j 1st p of each new r to last p preceding r cl—tie and cut.

1st Row—R, 3 ds, 7 p, sep by 2 ds, 3 ds, cl—ch 4 d, p, 4 ds—rep r, j 1st p to last p of last r—rep ch—rep r—s ch 4 ds—rep r—rep s ch—rep r 3 times and rep ch twice, j to opposite ch—1 ch, 5 p, sep by 6 ds, j center p to p of center figure—rep 1st row, j center, p 1st r, to center p, last r made—proceed around center figure, j all p of l ch to opposite p of preceding l ch—tie and cut.

Square Medallion No. 32

Crochet Cotton No. 50.

Center is composed of 4 clover leaves, sep by ch—r 3 p, sep by 3 ds, cl—rep r twice, j each to preceding r by 1st p—ch 9 ds, p, 9 ds—rep from beginning 3 times, j each clover leaf to preceding one on side and all to same p in center, tie and cut.

1st Row—Rep clover leaf, using 4 ds instead of 3 ds, j free p of center r to base of clover leaf (center figure) rep 1st ch—r 3 p, sep by 4 ds, j center p to p of ch (center figure)—turn—rep last r, without j—rep ch—rep 1st row around; tie and cut.

2d Row—Rep clover leaf of last row, j as before—ch 8 ds, p, 8 ds—r 6 ds, j to ch as last row—rep last ch—r 3 p, sep by 4 ds, j to center p of free r, last row—rep last ch—rep small r—rep ch—rep from 2nd row around; tie and cut.

CORNERS—Rep clover leaf, j on sides to p of ch nearest corner and j center p to base of single lr, last row.

Venetian Medallion No. 33

Crochet Cotton No, 40.

CENTER—R of 10 p, sep by 2 ds, cl.

1st Row—Ch of 2 ds, p, 2 ds, j shuttle thread to p of r leaving loop ½ inch—rep around, leaving sp between ch.

2d Row—R of 2 ds, j to p of ch (last row), 2 ds, cl—ch as before, j to sp between ch (last row), leaving ½ inch sp—rep around; tie and cut.

Butterfly Medallion No. 34

Crochet Cotton No. 60.

HEAD—R 9 ds, p (¼ inch), 5 ds, p as before, 9 ds, cl—

RIGHT SIDE OF BODY—7 ds, p, 7 ds.

LOWER PART OF BODY—R 3 p, sep by 6 ds, cl.

RIGHT WING—L ch 5 ds, j to p of last ch, 2 p, sep by 6 ds, 5 ds—r 11 p, sep by 2 ds, cl—rep l ch, making p instead of 6th p of last r, continue ch, 4 p, sep by 6 ds, j at base of lower r of body—ch 5 ds, j to 1st p in r of lower body.

LOWER RIGHT WING—R 5 ds, j to last p of continued l ch, 5 ds, 11 p, sep by 2 ds, cl—turn—ch 3 p, sep by 2 ds, j to 2nd p from last p of r—ch 6 p, sep by 1 ds, miss 1 p, j to next—ch 13 p, sep by 1 ds, j as last j—ch 6, p, sep by 1 ds—rep from last s ch 3 times, j as before. After completing last ch, j to 1st free p of l ch, upper wing, ch 6 ds, j to next p in l ch—r 6 p, sep by 2 ds, cl—ch 3 ds, j to l ch as before—rep last r and last ch 6, times, j each new r to preceding r by 1st p, and j ch as before where possible—add 3 ds to last ch, pass 1 thread over and 1 under at base of head.

LEFT SIDE OF BODY—Ch as for right side, j at end of opposite ch, rep right wing for left, tie and cut.

Small Medallion No. 35

Crochet Cotton No. 40.

CENTER—4 rings of 3 p, sep by 4 ds, j around, tie and cut.

1st Row—2 rings of 3 p, sep by 3 ds, j both rings in one p of center and each to other, sep r by s ch of 4 ds, p, 4 ds—ch 3 ds, 3 p, sep by 2 ds, 3 ds—r 3 p, sep by 3 ds—rep l ch—r 3 p, sep by 3 ds, j 2nd p to 3rd p of last r—r of 3 p, sep by 5 ds, 3 ds, cl—j 1st p to 2nd p of last r, j center p to p of center figure—r 3 p, sep by 3 ds, j to last r by 1st p—rep l ch—r of 3 p, sep by 3 ds, j to last r—rep l ch—rep around, tie and cut.

Medallion No. 36

Crochet Cotton No. 40.

CENTER—4 r of 3 p, sep by 4 ds, j 1st p of each r to 3rd p of preceding r, j 3rd p of 4th r to 1st p of 1st r, tie and cut.

1st Row—2 r of 3 p, sep by 3 ds, j 2nd p of each r to same p of center and j r together; sep r by ch of 4 ds, p, 4 ds. After 2nd r, ch of 3 ds, 3 p, sep by 2 ds, 3 ds—rep around, tie and cut.

2d Row—2 r of 3 p, sep by 4 ds, j 2nd p of both r to center p of s ch last row and j r together; sep r by ch of 4 ds, p, 4 ds— ch 3 ds, 3 p, sep by 2 ds, 3 ds—rep 2nd row around j to center p of l ch, tie and cut.

Triangular Medallion No. 37

Crochet Cotton No. 40.

CENTER—3 r of 4 p, sep by 4 ds, j r, tie and cut.

1st Row—2 r of 3 ds, p, 3 ds, j to left p of center, 4 ds, cl, (reading 2nd r backwards and sep r by ch of 3 ds, p, 3 ds) rep ch—rep r, j each pair of r to same p and the 2 pairs together—l ch of 3 ds, 5 p, sep by 2 ds, 3 ds—rep 1st row around, tie and cut.

2d Row—3 r of 3 p, sep by 3 ds, j center p of each r to p of one s ch; sep r by s ch of 3 ds, 3 p, sep by 2 ds, 3 ds. After 3rd r, ch as before, but make 4 p instead of 3. R as before, j to center p of l ch, last row.

CLOVER LEAF of 3 rings—1st and 3rd alike of 3 p, sep by 3 ds, j to ch and each to the other, add 1 ds on each side of 2nd p of center r—turn—directions given in paragraph above—rep, 4 p, ch; j 1st p to last p of clover leaf. Rep this row around, tie and cut.

Round Medallion No. 38

Crochet Cotton No. 40.

CENTER—R 5 p, sep by 2 ds, cl—ch 3 ds, 3 p, sep by 2 ds, 3 ds—rep r and ch 4 times, j each new r to preceding r by 2nd p, tie and cut.

1st Row—R 3 p, sep by 3 ds, j center p to 1st p of ch (center figure)—ch 2 ds, 5 p, sep by 1 ds, 2 ds—rep around, j r in groups of 3, one to a p, tie and cut.

2d Row—CLOVER LEAF—3 r of 3 p, sep by 3 ds, j 1st p of each new r to p of preceding r and j free p of center r to center p of ch, 1st row—l ch 6 ds, p, 6 ds—r, 3 p, sep by 3 ds, j center p to center of next ch—ch 4 ds, p, 4 ds—rep last r, j 1st p to last p of preceding r, and j center p to ch as before—rep l ch—rep 2nd row around, tie and cut.

Rose Medallion No. 39

Crochet Cotton No. 40.

CENTER OF ROSE—R, 1 ds, 6 p, sep by 2 ds, 1 ds, cl—tie and cut. Wind 2 yards from shuttle for ch thread.

FIRST ROW OF ROSE—Ch 7 ds, j to next p—rep around, j last time to 1st p—rep 1st row twice, adding 1 ds to 2nd row and 2 ds to 3rd row, j between ch preceding row—

LAST ROW OF ROSE—Ch 3 ds, p, 6 ds, p, 3 ds, j as before—rep this row around, tie and cut.

EDGE—**1st Row**—Sr, 3 ds, j to p of rose, 3 ds, cl—ch 3 p, sep by 2 ds. Rep this row around.

EDGE—**2d Row**—Rep sr, last row j to center p, of ch—ch 8 ds, p, 8 ds. Rep this row around, tie and cut.

Vine Medallion No. 40

Crochet Cotton No. 60.

CENTER—R 1 ds, 7 p, sep by 2 ds, 1 ds, cl—tie and cut.

1st Row—R 4 ds, j to p of center, 4 ds, cl—ch 5 p, sep by 2 ds—rep 1st row around, tie and cut.

2d Row—R 3 p, sep by 3 ds, j center p to corresponding p of ch (last row)—ch 4 p, sep by 2 ds, 5 ds, 4 p, sep by 2 ds—rep 2nd row around, tie and cut.

3d Row—R 2 p, sep by 6 ds, cl—rep r—ch 6 ds, j to 4th p of ch, last row 5 ds, j to next p of ch, 6 ds—rep r of this row, j to adjacent preceding r—rep r—turn—rep ch, this time the ch is on edge of Medallion. Rep around, j adjacent r, both upper and lower, tie and cut.

Medallion Collar and Square Yoke

COLLAR

Crochet Cotton No. 50.

CENTER—R 5 ds, p, 2 ds, p, 5 ds, cl—ch 4 ds, 3 p, sep by 2 ds, 4 ds—rep r, j 1st p of new r to last p of preceding r—rep ch—rep from 1st around until there are 6 r and 6 ch—j last r to 1st r made, tie and cut.

1st Row—R 6 ds, j to 1st p of ch (last row), 6 ds, cl—ch 4 ds, 3 p, sep by 2 ds, 4 ds—rep r, j to last p, same ch—rep ch—rep around, tie and cut.

YOKE

Crochet Cotton No. 60.

MEDALLION CENTER—R 20, p, sep by 1 ds, cl—tie and cut.

1st Row—Sr 4 ds, j to p of center, 4 ds, cl—sp (½ inch)—turn—lr, 3 ds, p, 2 ds, 3 p, sep by 1 ds, 2 ds, p, 3 ds, cl—sp as before—rep sr, j as before, sp—rep lr, j to preceding lr by 1st p—rep around—tie and cut.

SMALL MEDALLION FOR CENTER FRONT—Center Ring—10 p, sep by 1 ds, cl—tie and cut.

1st Row—Rep 1st row, large medallion, but do not j last lr to 1st lr.

MEDALLION CORNERS

Crochet Cotton No. 70.

CLOVER LEAF—1st r—4 ds, p, 4 ds, p, 2 p, sep by 2 ds, 4 ds, cl—2nd r—4 ds, j to last p preceding r, 4 ds, p, 2 p, sep by 2 ds, 4 ds, cl—3rd r—4 ds, j to last p of 2nd r, 2 p, sep by 2 ds, 4 ds, p, 4 ds, cl—l ch, 3 ds, 6 p, sep by 2 ds, 3 ds—sr, 4 ds, j to 1st p of 1st r, 4 ds, cl—rep ch—rep clover leaf, j 3rd p of 1st r to 2nd p, 1st r (preceding clover leaf); j 2nd p of center r to same p preceding center r and j each r of clover leaf to other as before—rep from l ch around without j ch to each other, tie and cut.

Edge of handkerchief is crocheted.

HANDKERCHIEF EDGE

Crochet Cotton No. 70.

Lr, 4 ds, 3 p, sep by 3 ds, 4 ds, 5 p, sep by 3 ds, 4 ds, cl—s ch 4 ds, p, 4 ds—sr. 4 ds, j to last p of lr, 4 ds, cl—rep from s ch 4 times—rep s ch, j to next p of lr—turn—l ch, 4 ds, 3 p sep by 2 ds, 4 ds—rep from beginning, j p of 1st s ch to p of opposite s ch.

WIDE EDGE

Crochet Cotton No. 100.

LARGE MEDALLION—C e n t e r Ring—18 p, sep by 1 ds.

1st Row—R 3 ds, 3 p, sep by 2 ds, 4 ds, cl—j at base of r to p of center—rep around until there are r at all p; join none.

2d Row—R 8 p, sep by 1 ds, cl—j at base of r to center p of r, (last row)—rep 2nd row around, j nothing, except at base of r—tie and cut.

SMALL MEDALLION—R 6 ds, 4 p sep by 2 ds, 6 ds, cl—rep r 4 times, j 1st p of each new r to last p of preceding r, and j last p of 5th r to 1st p of 1st r, tie and cut.

Any medallions of this book may be combined effectively for a handkerchief of this kind.

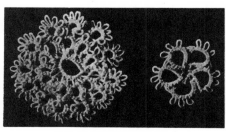

Detail of Wide Edge

Edgings

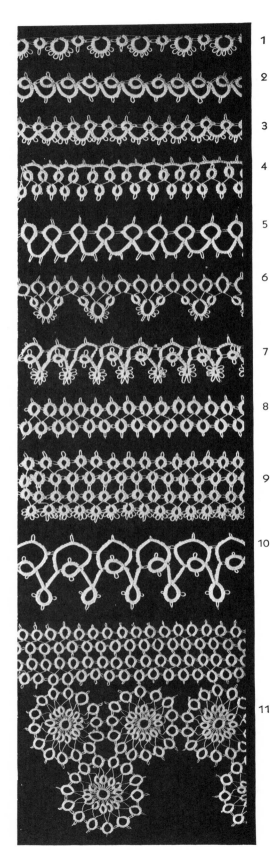

1
2
3
4
5
6
7
8
9
10
11

NOTE: There are many attractive possibilities in the edgings shown on this and the following page, from trimming dainty handkerchiefs to linens, chair sets, etc., and this use should determine the size thread needed. For handkerchiefs and dainty collars, either Nos. 70, 80, 90, or 100 SILKINE CROCHET COTTON, or STAR CROCHET COTTON, or SILKINE TATTING THREAD will be found appropriate. For coarser work, use sizes 10, 30, or 50. As will be seen, several were designed to combine a color and white, and many attractive tones will be found in either of the kinds mentioned above.

EDGING No. 1
(One Shuttle)

Sr 3 ds, 3 p sep by 3 ds, 3 ds, cl, sp, *lr 3 ds, j to third p of sr, 3 ds, 6 p sep by 2 ds, 3 ds, p, 3 ds, cl, sp, sr 3 ds, j to last p of lr, 3 ds, 2 p sep by 3 ds, 3 ds, cl. Repeat from *.

EDGING No. 2
(Two Shuttles)

*R 4 ds, 2 p sep by 4 ds, 8 ds, cl, ch 8 ds, p, 8 ds, j to second p of r, repeat from *.

EDGING No. 3
(Two Shuttles)

R 3 ds, 3 p sep by 3 ds, 3 ds, cl, *ch 3 ds, 3 p sep by 2 ds, 3 ds, r 3 ds, j to third p of r, 3 ds, 2 p sep by 3 ds, 3 ds, cl, repeat from *.

EDGING No. 4
(Two Shuttles)

R 6 ds, p, 6 ds, cl, sp, 6 ds, p, 6 ds, cl, sp, 6 ds, p, 6 ds, cl, repeat for the desired length. For p ch at top: join in p of first r, *ch 6 ds, p, 6 ds, sk 1 r, j in p of next r, repeat from *.

EDGING No. 5
(Two Shuttles)

R 6 ds, 3 p sep by 6 ds, 6 ds, cl, *ch 6 ds, p, 4 ds, p, 6 ds, r 6 ds, j to third p of r, 6 ds, 2 p sep by 6 ds, 6 ds, cl. Repeat from *.

POINTED EDGING No. 6
(One Shuttle)

R 5 ds, 3 p sep by 5 ds, 5 ds, cl, *sp, turn, sr 5 ds, p, 5 ds, cl, turn, sp, 5 ds, j to third p of r, 5 ds, 2 p sep by 5 ds, 5 ds, cl, turn, sp, lr 5 ds, j to p of sr, 7 p sep by 2 ds, 5 ds, cl, turn, sp, r 5 ds, j to p of opposite r, 5 ds, 2 p sep by 5 ds, 5 ds, cl, turn, sp, r 5 ds, j to last p of lr, 5 ds, cl, turn, sp, r 5 ds, j to third p of opposite r, 5 ds, 2 p sep by 5 ds, 5 ds, cl, repeat from *.

EDGING No. 7
(Two Shuttles)

R 3 ds, 3 p sep by 3 ds, 3 ds, cl, 1 ch 3 ds, 3 p sep by 3 ds, 3 ds, *j to center p of r, 3 ds, r 8 p sep by 1 ds, cl, ch 3 ds, r 3 ds, 3 p sep by 3 ds, 3 ds, cl, 1 ch 3 ds, j to last p of last 1 ch, 3 ds, 2 p sep by 3 ds, 3 ds, repeat from *

INSERTION No. 8
(One Shuttle)

R 4 ds, 3 p sep by 4 ds, 4 ds, cl, turn, sp, r 4 ds, 3 p sep by 4 ds, 4 ds, cl, *turn, sp, r 4 ds, j to third p of first r, 4 ds, 2 p sep by 4 ds, 4 ds, cl, turn, sp, r 4 ds, j to third p of second r, 4 ds, 2 p sep by 4 ds, 4 ds, cl, repeat from *.

EDGING TO MATCH No. 9
(One Shuttle)

Make top row like insertion, using only 3 ds instead of 4 ds, for rings. **2d row:** R 3 ds, p, 3 ds, j to center p of r on top row, 3 ds, p, 3 ds, cl, turn, sp, r 3 ds, 6 p sep by 1 ds, 3 ds, cl, *turn, sp, r 3 ds, j to p of first r, 3 ds, j to next p on heading row, 3 ds, p, 3 ds, cl, turn, sp, r 3 ds, j to sixth p of r 5 p sep by 1 ds, 3 ds, cl. Repeat.

EDGING No. 10
(Two Shuttles)

R 6 ds, 3 p sep by 6 ds, 6 ds, cl, 1 ch 8 ds, 3 p sep by 8 ds, 8 ds, *j to center p of r, 8 ds, r 6 ds, 3 p sep by 6 ds, 6 ds, cl, ch 8 ds, r 6 ds, 3 p sep by 6 ds, 6 ds, cl, ch 8 ds, j to third p of 1 ch, 8 ds, 2 p sep by 8 ds, repeat from *.

POINTED EDGING No. 11
(One Shuttle)

1st row: R 4 ds, 3 p sep by 4 ds, 4 ds, cl, sp, turn, r 4 ds, 3 p sep by 4 ds, 4 ds, cl, *turn, sp, r 4 ds, j to third p of first r, 4 ds, 2 p sep by 4 ds, 4 ds, cl, turn, sp, r 4 ds, j to third p of second r, 4 ds, 2 p sep by 4 ds, 4 ds, cl, repeat from * across. Repeat first row, joining center p on one side of row to p on first row. **Medallions:** R 14 p sep by 2 ds, cl, sr 8 ds, j to p of center r, 8 ds, cl, sp, turn, lr 6 ds, 3 p sep by 6 ds, 6 ds, cl, *turn, sp, r 8 ds, j to next p on center r, 8 ds, cl, turn, sp, 6 ds, j to third p of lr, 6 ds, 2 p sep by 6 ds, 6 ds, cl, repeat from * around, j to center p of last 2 r to p of 2 r on heading. Join next medallion to first, sk 2 p on first medallion, j to next r, sk 4 r on heading, j in next 2 p, j a medallion between first 2 medallions to form point.

EDGING No. 12

R 3 ds, 5 p sep by 2 ds, 3 ds, cl, *ch 6 ds, r 6 ds, j to fifth p of last r, 2 ds, 4 p sep by 2 ds, 6 ds, cl, r 7 p, ch 6 ds, r 3 ds, j to fifth p of last r, 2 ds, 4 p sep by 2 ds, 3 ds, cl, repeat from * for desired length.

FORGET-ME-NOT TATTED EDGING No. 13

Make all rings pink. R 9 p, cl, (white) 1 ch 6 ds, 3 p *sep by 6 ds, 6 ds, j to fifth p of r, 6 ds, r 9 p, cl, ch 6 ds, r 9 p, cl, 1 ch 6 ds, j to p on opposite 1 ch, 6 ds, 2 p, repeat from * for desired length.

EDGING (White) No. 14

R 3 ds, 5 p sep by 2 ds, 3 ds, cl, 1 ch 5 ds, p, *5 ds, 6 p sep by 2 ds, 5 ds, p, 5 ds, r 3 ds, 2 p sep by 2 ds, 2 ds, j to center p of last r, 2 ds, 2 p sep by 2 ds, 3 ds, cl, (ch 4 ds, r 3 ds, j to last p of last r, 2 ds, 4 p sep by 2 ds, 3 ds, cl) twice, 1 ch 5 ds, j to p on opposite 1 ch; repeat from * for desired length.

EDGING No. 15

R 4 ds, 3 p sep by 3 ds, 4 ds, cl, lr 5 ds, j to 3 p of last r, 2 ds, 6 p sep by 2 ds, 5 ds, cl *r 4 ds, j to last p of lr, 3 ds, p, 3 ds, p, 4 ds, cl, ch 4 ds, 3 p sep by 2 ds, 4 ds, r 4 ds, p, 3 ds, j to center p of last r, 3 ds, p, 4 ds, cl, r 4 ds, 3 p sep by 3 ds, 4 ds, cl, ch 9 ds, r 4 ds, p, 3 ds, j to fifth free p of lr, 3 ds, p, 4 ds, cl, r 4 ds, 3 p sep by 3 ds, 4 ds, cl, ch 9 ds, lr, 5 ds, j to center p of last r, 2 ds, 6 p sep by 2 ds, 5 ds, cl, ch 9 ds, r 4 ds, p, 3 ds, j to last p of lr, 3 ds, p, 4 ds, cl, r 4 ds, 3 p sep by 3 ds, 4 ds, cl, ch 9 ds, r 4 ds, p, 3 ds, j to center p of opposite r, 3 ds, p, 4 ds, cl, r 4 ds, 3 p sep by 3 ds, 4 ds, cl, ch 4 ds, 3 p sep by 2 ds, 4 ds, r 4 ds, p, 3 ds, j to center p of last r, 3 ds, p, 4 ds, cl, lr 5 ds, j to third p of last r, 2 ds, j to center p of opposite r, 2 ds, 5 p sep by 2 ds, 5 ds, cl, repeat from * for desired length.

EDGING (Blue and White) No. 16

Make all rings blue, lr 12 p, cl, with white thread ch 4 ds, 3 p sep by 2 ds, 4 ds, *sr 4 ds, j to tenth p of lr, 1 ch, 4 ds, 7 p sep by 2 ds, 4 ds, sr 4 ds, j in same p with last sr, 4 ds, cl, (ch 4 ds, 3 p sep by 2 ds, 4 ds, sk 2 p of lr, j in next p, 5 ds), sr 4 ds, 4 ds, cl, ch 5 ds, lr 12 p, cl, ch 4 ds, p, 2 ds, j in center p of opposite ch, 2 ds, p, 4 ds, repeat from * for desired length.
Heading: *Sr 4 ds, j in fourth p of lr, 4 ds, cl, ch 4 ds, 3 p sep by 2 ds, 4 ds, j in p of sr of last row, ch 4 ds, 3 p sep by 2 ds, 4 ds, repeat from * across.

SHAMROCK EDGING (Yellow and White) No. 17—Two Shuttles

Rings are all yellow, ch white.
Sr 3 ds, 5 p sep by 2 ds, 3 ds, cl, *1 ch 8 ds, p, 2 ds, p, 8 ds, 2 p sep by 2 ds, 8 ds, lr 6 ds, 2 p sep by 2 ds, 2 ds, j to fourth p of sr, 2 ds, 2 p sep by 2 ds, 6 ds, cl, (lr 6 ds, j to fifth p of lr, 2 ds, 4 p sep by 2 ds, 6 ds, cl) 2 times, 1 ch 8 ds, 2 p sep by 2 ds, 8 ds, **lr 6 ds, 2 p sep by 2 ds, 2 ds, j to center p of last lr, 2 ds, 2 p sep by 2 ds, 6 ds, cl, (lr 6 ds, j to last p of lr, 2 ds, 4 p sep by 2 ds, 6 ds, cl) 2 times, ch 8 ds, repeat from **three times, to first p on opposite ch, 2 ds, j to second p of same ch, 8 ds, Make another shamrock and join as others are joined, 1 ch 8 ds, j to the picots on opposite ch as before, 8 ds, 2 p sep by 2 ds, 8 ds, sr 3 ds, p, 2 ds, j to center p of last lr, 2 ds, 3 p sep by 2 ds, 3 ds, cl, ch 6 ds, 2 p sep by 2 ds, 6 ds, sr 3 ds, p, 2 ds, j to fourth p of last r, 2 ds, 3 p sep by 2 ds, 3 ds, cl. Repeat from * for desired length, joining the shamrocks on sides together by center picots.

TATTED SCARF ENDS No. 18

Heading: Lr 5 ds, 5 p sep by 2 ds, 5 ds, cl, sp (¼-inch), turn, *sr, 4 ds, lp, 4 ds, cl, sp, turn, lr 5 ds, j to fifth p of last lr, 2 ds, 4 p sep by 2 ds, 5 ds, cl, sp, turn, sr 4 ds, j in lp of last sr, 4 ds, cl, sp, turn, lr 5 ds, j to fifth p of last lr, 2 ds, 4 p sep by 2 ds, 5 ds, cl, repeat from * for desired length. Fasten off. Repeat for other side of insertion joining 2 sr in lp with 1 sr of first row.
Medallions: R 14 p, cl, tie and cut, lr 6 ds, 5 p sep by 2 ds, 6 ds, cl, sp (¼-inch ch), turn, sr 4 ds, j in a p of center ring, 4 ds, cl, *sp, turn, lr 6 ds, j to fifth p of lr, 2 ds, 4 p sep by 2 ds, 6 ds, cl, sp, turn, sr 4 ds, j in next p of center r, 4 ds, cl, repeat from * around, joining center p of 3 lr to 3 lr of heading—and skipping 1 r of medallion, join 2 r of each medallion. Skip 2 rings on heading between medallions.

EDGING (Scarf End) No. 19

Make all r of a color and the ch white.
Motif: R 7 lp, cl, tie and cut. *R 4 ds, j to lp of r, 4 ds, cl, ch 7 ds, 3 p sep by 2 ds, 7 ds, repeat from * around, tie and cut. Make desired number of motifs—then make scallops as follows: *R 5 ds, 5 p sep by 2 ds, 5 ds, cl, ch 7 ds, (r 2 ds, 3 p sep by 2 ds, 2 ds, j to center p of ch on motif, 2 ds, 3 p sep by 2 ds, 2 ds, cl, ch 9 ds, 5 p sep by 2 ds, 9 ds) 2 times, r 2 ds, 3 p sep by 2 ds, 2 ds, j to center p of next ch on motif, 2 ds, 3 p sep by 2 ds, 2 ds, cl, r 2 ds, 7 p sep by 2 ds, 2 ds, cl, (ch 9 ds, 5 p sep by 2 ds, 9 ds, r 2 ds, 3 p sep by 2 ds, 2 ds, j to center p of next ch, 2 ds, 3 p sep by 2 ds, 2 ds, cl) 2 times, ch 7 ds, repeat from * for each scallop.
Heading: R 4 ds, j to center p of first r, 4 ds, cl, *ch 8 ds, 3 p sep by 2 ds, 8 ds, r 4 ds, j to center p of motif ch, 4 ds, cl, ch 5 ds, 3 p sep by 2 ds, 5 ds, r 4 ds, j to center p of next ch, 4 ds, cl, ch 8 ds, 3 p sep by 2 ds, 8 ds, r 4 ds, j to center p of r, 4 ds, cl, repeat from * across.

(Continued on page 31)

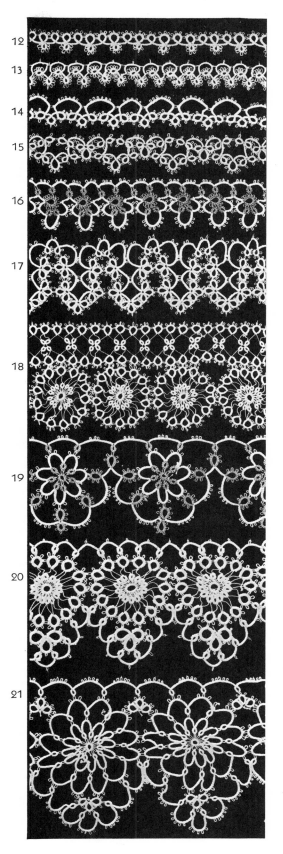

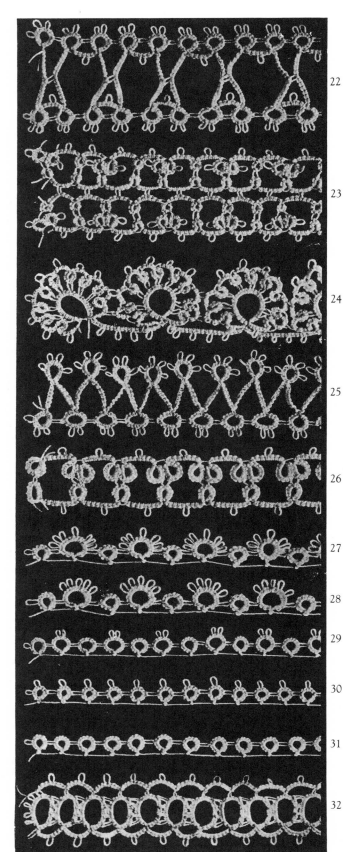

22

23

24

25

26

27

28

29

30

31

32

Beading No. 22

Crochet Cotton No. 40.

R, 4 ds, p, 3 ds, p, 2 ds, p, 3 ds, p, 4 ds, cl—l ch, 7 ds, p, 7 ds—rep r—s ch, 3 ds, p, 3 ds—rep r, j 1st p of new r to last p of 2nd r—rep l ch, j p to p of last l ch—rep r, j to p of 1st r—rep s ch—rep from beginning to desired length.

Beading or Insertion No. 23

Crochet Cotton No. 40.

1st Row—R, 3 ds, p, 3 ds, cl—ch 3 ds, p, 3 ds—rep to desired length.

2d Row—R, 3 ds, p, 3 ds, j to p of 1st r of 1st row, 3 ds, cl—rep, backwards last r, j to same p with last r—ch 3 ds, p 3 ds—r 3 ds, j to 2nd r of 1st row, 3 ds, cl—rep ch—rep 2nd row to end of 1st row—rep 1st row, j ch to p of ch (1st row)—rep 2nd row to end.

Peacock Edging No. 24

Crochet Cotton No. 40.

Lr 9 p, sep by 3 ds, cl—ch 3 ds, p, 3 ds—r 3 ds, j into last p of lr, 3 ds, cl—ch 2 ds, p, 2 ds—rep around lr—ch 4 p, sep by 4 ds—j at base of lr—rep fans, j 2nd and 3rd s ch to 8th and 9th of last fan.

Edging No. 25 to Match No. 22

Crochet Cotton No. 40.

R 4 ds, p, 3 ds, p, 2 ds, p, 3 ds, p, 4 ds, cl—ch 7ds—rep r—rep ch—rep r, j 1st p of 3rd r to 4th p of 1st r—rep to desired length, j r on only one side. This edge will fit curved edges nicely.

Beading No. 26

Crochet Cotton No. 30.

1st Row—R 6 ds, p, 6 ds, cl—ch 4 ds, p, 5 ds—rep to desired length.

2d Row—R 8 ds, j to p of r of 1st row, 4 ds, cl—rep r, (reading backwards)—ch 4 ds, p, 4 ds—rep to end of first row.

Edging No. 27

Crochet Cotton No. 30.

FIRST RING—3 ds, p, 5 ds, p, 3 ds, cl—tie, sp. SECOND RING—3 ds, j in last p of preceding r, 3 p, sep by 1 ds, 3 ds, p, 3 ds, 4 p, sep by 1 ds, 3 ds, cl—tie—rep to desired length, j each new r to preceding r.

Edging No. 28

Crochet Cotton No. 30.

FIRST RING—3 ds, p, 7 ds, p, 3 ds, cl—tie—sp. SECOND RING—3 ds, j in last p of preceding r, 3 ds, 5 p, sep by 2 ds, 3 ds, p, 3 ds, cl—tie—rep to desired length, j each new r to preceding r.

Edging No. 29

Crochet Cotton No. 60.

FIRST RING—4 ds, p, 8 ds, p, 4 ds, cl—sp. SECOND RING—4 ds, j to last p of preceding r, 4 ds, p, 2 ds, p, 4 ds, cl—tie—rep to desired length, j each new r to preceding r.

Edging No. 30

Crochet Cotton No. 60.

R 3 p, sep by 4 ds, cl—tie—sp—rep r, j 1st p of each new r to last p of preceding r—rep to desired length.

Baldhead Edging No. 31

Crochet Cotton No. 60.

R 4 ds, p, 7 ds, p, 4 ds, cl—tie—sp—r as before, j 1st p of each new r to last p of preceding r—rep to desired length.

Beading No. 32

Crochet Cotton No. 40.

1st Row—R 9 p, sep by 3 ds, cl—working close to r, ch 4 ds, p, 4 ds—r as before, j 4 first p of each new r to 4 last p of preceding r—rep ch after each new r, rep to desired length.

2d Row—Tie shuttle thread to center p of end r, and working from left to right make ch as before, j to center p of each r.

Insertions and Edgings

Edging or Beading No. 33

Crochet Cotton No. 30.

R 4 ds, 5 p, sep by 3 ds, 4 ds, p, 4 ds, 5 p, sep by 3 ds, 4 ds, cl—tie, rep to desired length, j 5 first p of each new r to 5 last p of preceding r.

Beading No. 34

Crochet Cotton No. 30.

1st Row—R 3 ds, p, 3 ds, cl—ch 4 ds, p, 4 ds, bringing first ds close to r, rep to desired length.

2d Row—Rep 1st row, j each p of r to p of r of last row—rep to end of 1st row.

Edging No. 35

Crochet Cotton No. 30.

R 4 ds, 3 p, sep by 3 ds, 4 ds, p, 4 ds, 3 p, sep by 3 ds, 4 ds, cl—tie—rep to desired length, j 3 first p of each new r to 3 last p of each preceding r.

Edging No. 36

Crochet Cotton No. 30.

First Ring—6 ds, p, 6 ds, cl—ch 6 ds, p, 6 ds.

Second Ring—Rep 1st r, but j to p of last r instead of making p—turn—rep 1st r—turn—rep ch, rep 2nd r—rep from beginning to desired length.

Edging No. 37

Crochet Cotton No. 30.

First Ring—8 p, sep by 1 ds, cl—ch 6 ds, p, 6 ds.

Second Ring—6 ds, j to 4th p of 1st r, 6 ds, cl—rep 2nd r, making p where it j—turn—rep ch—rep 1st r, j 4th p to p of preceding r—rep from beginning to desired length

Edging No. 38

Crochet Cotton No. 40.

First Ring—3 ds, 6 p, sep by 2 ds, 3 ds, cl—l ch 7 ds, p, 7 ds.

Second Ring—6 ds, j to last p of 1st r, 6 ds, cl—s ch, 3 ds—rep 2nd r, j to next p of 1st r—rep 2nd r, making p instead of j—rep same again—rep s ch—rep last r, j to base of 2nd r made—rep l ch—rep from beginning to desired length, j 1st r to 2 preceding sr, by 1st and 2nd p.

Edging No. 39 to Match Medallion No. 30 (p. 20)

Crochet Cotton No. 40.

First Ring—3 p, sep by 3 ds, cl—ch, 3 p, sep by 3 ds—rep r, j 1st p to last p of preceding r, leaving 2 p free—rep ch—rep r, j 2 1st p to 2 of last r—rep ch—rep r, j 1st p to remaining p of last r, and j 2nd p to corresponding p of 1st r—rep ch—rep from beginning. Always j center p of 1st new ch to corresponding p of opposite ch.

Edging No. 40

Crochet Cotton No. 30.

First Ring—6 ds, p, 6 ds, cl—rep 1st r—l ch 4 ds, p, 6 ds, p, 6 ds, p, 4 ds, j to p of last r, continue ch, p, 6 ds—2nd r, 7 p, sep by 1 ds, cl—ch 6 ds—rep from beginning, always j p of 1st new r to last p of preceding l ch, j new ch to last ch by 1st p. Insertion to match may be easily made by repeating the edge and j the p r between, or in center.

Insertion No. 41

Crochet Cotton No. 30.

Clover Leaf—First Ring—2 p, sep by 5 ds, cl—

Second Ring—3 p, sep by 5 ds, j 1st p to last p of preceding r—rep 1st r, j as in 2nd r—ch 8 p, sep by 4 ds—rep from beginning, j 1st p of new r to last p of ch and j 3rd p of new ch to free p of center r, of preceding clover leaf.

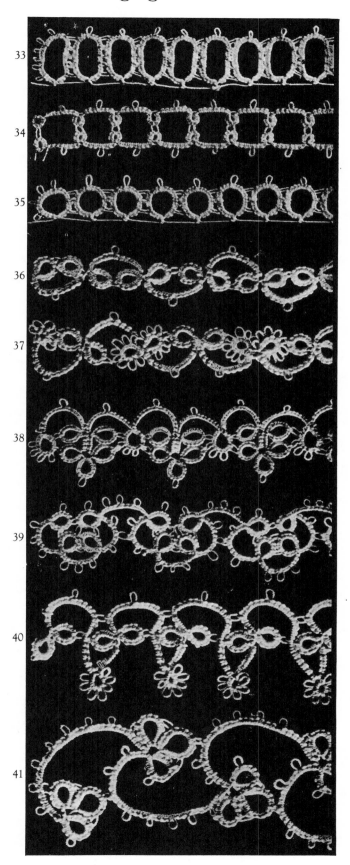

33

34

35

36

37

38

39

40

41

Edgings

Edging No. 42

Crochet Cotton No. 30.

FIRST RING—2 p, sep by 5 ds, cl.

SECOND RING—5 ds, j to p of last r, 6 ds, p, 6 ds, p, 5 ds, cl—rep 1st r, j to last p of preceding r—tie by passing thread through p where 2 last r j—ch 6 ds, p, 6 ds—rep from beginning, j 1st p of 1st new r to center p of large r, of last clover leaf. Insertion may be made by making p on both edges.

Edging No. 43

Crochet Cotton No. 30.

R 3 p, sep by 4 ds, cl.

FIRST CHAIN—3 p, sep by 2 ds—r, 5 ds, j to last p of 1st r, 5 ds, cl—rep 1st ch—rep last r, j in same p as before—rep 1st ch, j in 2nd p of 1st r—ch 5 ds, p, 5 ds—r 3 p, sep by 3 ds, j 1st p to center p of last 3 p ch—rep last ch, j as illustrated—rep from beginning to desired length.

Basket Edging No. 44

Crochet Cotton No. 40.

FIRST RING—4 p, sep by 2 ds, cl—l ch, 2 p, sep by 4 ds—

SECOND RING—5 p, sep by 2 ds, j 2nd p to 3rd p of last r, cl—rep 2nd r 4 times, sep them by s ch of 3 ds, and j 1st p of each new r to last p of preceding r—l ch 4 ds, j to last p of preceding ch, continue ch, 4 ds, p, 4 ds—rep 1st r, j 2nd p to 4th p of last r— rep l ch—rep 2nd r 3 times, sep, by ch of 4 ds, and j 2nd p of 1st new r to 3rd p of preceding r, leaving two next r free—rep from beginning to desired length.

Edging No. 45

Crochet Cotton No. 40.

FIRST RING—8 ds, p, 8 ds, cl—l ch, 5 p, sep by 4 ds, j to p of 1st r, continue ch, 5 ds.

SECOND RING—8 p, sep by 2 ds, cl—s ch, 5 ds—rep to desired length, j 1st p in each new l ch to last p in each preceding l ch.

Nos. 46 and 47 —Directions on opposite page.

42
43
44
45
46
47

Edgings and Their Uses

Towel
Crochet Cotton No. 30.

CENTER—R, 6 ds, 1 p, 6 ds, cl—ch 4 ds, 3 p, sep by 2 ds, 4 ds—r 6 ds, j to p of 1st r, 6 ds, cl—rep from beginning until you have 6 of each, tie, cut.

1st Row—R, 6 ds, j to 1st p of ch of center, 6 ds, cl—ch 3 ds, 3 p, sep by 2 ds, 3 ds—rep r, j to 3rd p of same ch—rep from beginning of this row until there are 10 r, leaving 1 free ch—rep medallions to desired length, j by opposite ch.

Pillowcase
Crochet Cotton No. 30.

FIRST RING—2 p, sep by 4 ds, cl—l ch 8 ds, p, 8 ds, p, 4 ds.

SECOND RING—3 p, sep by 3 ds, cl—s ch 8 ds, j to p of 1st r, 8 ds, rep 2nd r, j by 1st p to last p of preceding r—rep s ch and 2nd r until there are 5 ch and 6 r, j as before and j last r to 1st r—rep l ch, (reading backwards), j 1st p to 2nd p of l ch—rep from beginning, j 1st p of 1st r to p of last s ch made.

Rose Edging No. 46
(Illustrated on opposite page)
Crochet Cotton No. 60.

CENTER RING—11 p, sep by 3 ds, cl—sp all sp ¼ inch)—sr 6 ds, j to p of center r—sp—turn—lr 4 ds, 8 p, sep by 2 ds—rep from sr 7 times, j 1st p of each new lr to last p of preceding lr, and leaving only 3 free p on center r, tie and cut. Make enough medallions for length, crochet straightening line.

Medallion Edging No. 47
(Illustrated on opposite page)
Crochet Cotton No. 60.

CENTER RING OF MEDALLION—12 p, sep by 3 ds, cl—sp, ¼ inch—(all sps the same)—sr, 6 ds, j to p of center r, 6 ds, cl—sp—turn—lr 6 ds, 9 p, sep by 2 ds, 6 ds, cl—rep from sr around center, j 1st p of each new lr to last p of preceding lr—tie—j last lr to 1st lr cut. Make medallions separate.

FILLING—J to 5th p, lr—ch 7 ds, p, 7 ds, j to center p of next lr—rep twice—ch 7 ds—r, 4 p, sep by 5 ds, making 4th p ¼ inch—ch 7 ds, j to center p of next lr, 7 ds, j to lp of last r, 7 ds, j as before to lr—ch 5 ds, p, 5 ds—r, 5 ds, 5 p, sep by 2 ds, 5 ds, cl—rep last ch, j new medallion as before—ch 7 ds, j in p of opposite ch, 7 ds, j to next lr—rep last ch twice, j to lp of r, j to next p, same r, and j as before to new medallion—rep filling.

Dainty Gown Yoke

The lacy yoke shown may be made of No. 90 STAR CRO-CHET COTTON, or SILKINE CROCHET COTTON, and two shuttles. Requires 2 balls.

Medallions: R 4 ds, 5 p sep by 2 ds, 4 ds, cl, *ch 4 ds, 3 p sep by 2 ds, 4 ds, r 4 ds, p, 2 ds, j to fourth p of last r, 2 ds, 3 p sep by 2 ds, 4 ds, cl, repeat from * until there are 12 rings and 12 chs, join to first r and first ch.   Tie and cut.

Make 27 medallions (for 36-inch bust), j each together by the center p of 2 chs.

For insertion on lower edge: R 4 ds, 2 p sep by 2 ds, 2 ds, i to center p of second free ch on medallion, 2 ds, 2 p sep by 2 ds, 4 ds, cl, sp (⅛-inch), turn, *sr 4 ds, lp, 4 ds, cl, sp, turn, r 4 ds, j to last p of r, 2 ds, 4 p sep by 2 ds, 4 ds, cl, sp, turn, sr 4 ds, j in lp of sr, 4 ds, cl, sp, turn, r 4 ds, j to last p of r,

2 ds, p, 2 ds, j in center p of next ch, 2 ds, 2 p sep by 2 ds, 4 ds, cl, repeat from * around, making 3 rings between each medallion.   Make other side of insertion like one just made.

Top Edging: R 4 ds, 2 p sep by 2 ds, 2 ds, j to center p of second ch of medallion, 2 ds, 2 p sep by 2 ds, 4 ds, cl, sp, turn, *sr 4 ds, p, 4 ds, cl, sp, turn, r 4 ds, j to last p of r, 2 ds, 4 p sep by 2 ds, 4 ds, cl, sp, turn, r 4 ds, j to sr, 2 ds, 4 p sep by 2 ds, 6 ds, cl, sp, turn, r 4 ds, j to last r, 2 ds, p, 2 ds, j to center p of next ch, 2 ds, 2 p sep by 2 ds, 4 ds, cl, sp, turn, sr 4 ds, j to last p of lr, 4 ds, cl, sp, turn, r 4 ds, j to last r, 2 ds, 4 p sep by 2 ds, 4 ds, cl, repeat from * around, making 3 rings between each medallion.

Make 9 medallions for each shoulder strap and edge them on both sides with first row of the insertion.

DIRECTIONS FOR MEDALLIONS
(Continued from page 17)

3 ds, j to third p of sr, 2 ds, p, 2 ds, j to center p of ch (last row), 2 ds, p, 2 ds, p, 3 ds, cl, sr 3 ds, j to fifth p of lr, 3 ds, 2 p sep by 3 ds, 3 ds, cl, ch 10 ds, 3 p sep by 2 ds, 10 ds, repeat from * around.   Tie and cut.

ROUND MEDALLION No. 12
(Two Shuttles)

Center motif: (R 4 ds, 5 p sep by 3 ds, 4 ds, cl) 4 times, j r together by first and last p. Tie and cut. **1st row:** Join thread in center p of r (center motif) *ch 5 ds, 3 p sep by 2 ds, 5 ds, j in center p of next r, repeat from * around. Tie and cut. **2d row:** *R 6 ds, 5 p sep by 3 ds, 6 ds, cl, j to first p of ch (last row), l ch 10 ds, p, 10 ds, p, 10 ds, j in first p of l ch, 10 ds, sk 1 p on ch (last row), j in next p, r 6 ds, 5 p sep by 3 ds, 6 ds, cl, l ch 10 ds, p, 10 ds, p, 10 ds, j in first p of l ch, 10 ds, repeat from * around. Tie and cut. **3d row:** Join thread to center p of l ch (last row), *ch 6 ds, 3 p sep by 3 ds, 6 ds, j in center p of ring, ch 6 ds, 3 p sep by 3 ds, 6 ds, j in p of l ch, repeat from * around. Tie and cut.

LARGE ROUND MEDALLION No. 13
(Two Shuttles)

Center motif: 8 r, (3 ds, 3 p sep by 3 ds, 3 ds, cl) j to-gether by first and last p. Tie and cut. **1st row:** Sr 3 ds, p, 3 ds, j to p of center motif, 3 ds, p, 3 ds, cl, r 3 ds, 3 p sep by 3 ds, 3 ds, cl, ch 9 ds, (lr 9 ds, j to p of sr, 3 ds, j to next p of center motif, 3 ds, p, 9 ds, cl, r 9 ds, 3 p sep by 3 ds, 9 ds, cl, ch 9 ds, sr 3 ds, j to last p of lr, 3 ds, 2 p sep by 3 ds,

3 ps, cl, sr 3 ds, 3 p sep by 3 ds, 3 ds, cl, ch 9 ds) 5 times, lr 9 ds, j to third p of sr, 3 ds, j to next p of center motif, 3 ds, j to first p of first sr, 9 ds, cl, lr 9 ds, 3 p sep by 3 ds, 9 ds, cl, ch 9 ds, tie and cut. **2d row:** *R 8 ds, p, 2 ds, j in center p of sr, 2 ds, p, 8 ds, cl, ch 6 ds, 5 p sep by 3 ds, 6 ds, j in center p of lr, 6 ds, 5 p sep by 3 ds, 6 ds, repeat from * around. Tie and cut.

LARGE SQUARE MEDALLION No. 14

For small motif: R 12 ds, lp, 12 ds, cl, (ch 7 ds, 3 p sep by 2 ds, 7 ds, r 12 ds, j in lp, 12 ds, cl) 3 times, ch 7 ds, 3 p sep by 2 ds, 7 ds, j to first ch.   Tie and cut.   Make 3 more motifs like one just made.   Join center p of ch of first motif to center p of ch of second motif together.   Join next 2 so they form a square.   **Outer edge:** *(R 6 ds, j to first p to right on ch (last row), 6 ds, cl, turn, ch 6 ds, 3 p sep by 2 ds, 6 ds, turn, r 6 ds, sk 1 p on same ch, j in next p, 6 ds, cl, ch 6 ds, 3 p, 6 ds) 2 times, (r 6 ds, j in next p, 6 ds, cl) 2 times, ch 6 ds, j in p of opposite ch, 2 ds, 2 p sep by 2 ds, 6 ds, repeat from * around. Tie and cut.

LARGE ROUND MEDALLION No. 15
(Two Shuttles)

Center motif: 4 lr (6 ds, 6 p sep by 3 ds, 6 ds, cl) j r together by first and last p. Tie and cut. **1st row:** *R 5 ds, j to p on lr, 5 ds, cl, ch 5 ds, p, 5 ds, repeat from * all around. Tie and cut. **2d row:** *Sr 5 ds, j to p of ch (last row), 5 ds, cl, ch 8 ds, turn, r 3 ds, 3 p sep by 3 ds, 3 ds, cl, (r 3 ds, j to last p of last r, 3 ds, 2 p sep by 3 ds, 3 ds, cl) 2 times, ch 8 ds, turn, repeat from * around.   Tie and cut.

DIRECTIONS FOR MEDALLIONS

(Continued from page 18)

ONE-HALF SQUARE MEDALLION No. 25
(Two Shuttles)

R 4 ds, p, 5 ds, p, 4 ds, cl, ch 6 ds, p, 6 ds, p, 6 ds, r 4 ds, j to p of last r, 5 ds, p, 4 ds, cl, ch 6 ds, r 4 ds, p, 5 ds, p, 4 ds, cl, ch 6 ds, r 4 ds, p, 5 ds, p, 4 ds, cl, ch 6 ds, j to p of ch opposite, 6 ds, p, 6 ds, r 4 ds, j to p of last r, 5 ds, p, 4 ds, cl, ch 6 ds, p, 6 ds, p, 6 ds, r 4 ds, j to p of last r, 5 ds, p, 4 ds, cl, ch 6 ds, p, 6 ds, p, 6 ds, r 4 ds, j to p of last r, 5 ds, j to p of r opposite, 4 ds, cl, ch 6 ds, r 4 ds, j to p of opposite r, 5 ds, p, 4 ds, cl, ch 6 ds, r 4 ds, p, 5 ds, p, 4 ds, cl, ch 6 ds, j to p of ch, 6 ds, p, 6 ds, r 4 ds, j to p of last r, 5 ds, p, 4 ds, cl, ch 6 ds, r 4 ds, p, 5 ds, p, 4 ds, cl, ch 6 ds, j to p of ch opposite, 6 ds, p, 6 ds, r 4 ds, j to p of last r, 5 ds, p, 4 ds, cl, ch 6 ds, r 4 ds, p, 5 ds, p, 4 ds, cl, ch 6 ds, j to p of opposite ch, 6 ds, j to p of opposite ch, 6 ds, r 4 ds, j to p of last r, 5 ds, p, 4 ds, cl, ch 6 ds, j to p of ch opposite, 6 ds, p, 6 ds, r 4 ds, j to p of last r, 5 ds, p, 4 ds, cl, ch 6 ds, p, 6 ds, p, 6 ds, r 4 ds, j to p of last r, 5 ds, j to p of opposite r, 4 ds, cl, ch 6 ds, r 4 ds, j to p of opposite r, 5 ds, p, 4 ds, cl, ch 6 ds, r 4 ds, p, 5 ds, p, 4 ds, cl, ch 6 ds, j to p of opposite ch, 6 ds, p, 6 ds, r 4 ds, j to p of last r, 5 ds, p, 4 ds, cl, ch 6 ds, p, 6 ds, p, 6 ds, r 4 ds, j to p of last r, 5 ds, j to p of opposite r, 4 ds, cl, ch 6 ds, r 4 ds, j to p of opposite r, 5 ds, p, 4 ds, cl, ch 6 ds, r 4 ds, p, 5 ds, p, 4 ds, cl, ch 6 ds, j to p of opposite ch, 6 ds, p, 6 ds, r 4 ds, j to p of last r, 5 ds, p, 4 ds, cl, ch 6 ds, p, 6 ds, p, 6 ds, r 4 ds, j to p of last r, 5 ds, j to p of opposite r, 4 ds, cl, ch 6 ds, r 4 ds, j to p of opposite r, 5 ds, p, 4 ds, cl, ch 6 ds, p, 5 ds, p, 4 ds, cl, ch 6 ds, j to p of opposite ch, 6 ds, p, 6 ds, r 4 ds, j to p of last r, 5 ds, p, 4 ds, cl, ch 6 ds, j to p of opposite ch, 6 ds, p, 6 ds, r 4 ds, j to p of last r, 5 ds, p, 4 ds, cl, ch 6 ds, p, 6 ds, p, 6 ds, r 4 ds, j to p of last r, 5 ds, p, 4 ds, cl.

TATTED SQUARE MEDALLION No. 26
(Two Shuttles)

Center: R 7 ds, 6 p sep by 3 ds, 7 ds, cl, (r 7 ds, j to sixth p of last r, 3 ds, 5 p sep by 3 ds, 7 ds, cl) 3 times. Join last r to first r by first and last p. Tie and cut. **1st row:** *R 5 ds, j to p of center motif, 5 ds, cl, turn, ch 5 ds, p, 5 ds, turn. Repeat from * around. Tie and cut. **2d row:** *R 3 ds, 3 p sep by 3 ds, 3 ds, cl, r 3 ds, j in third p of last r, 3 ds, p, 3 ds, j to p of ch that comes in the center over large r in center motif, 3 ds, 2 p sep by 3 ds, 3 ds, cl, r 3 ds, j to fifth p of last r, 3 ds, 2 p sep by 3 ds, 3 ds, cl, (turn, ch 5 ds, 3 p sep by 2 ds, 5 ds, turn, r 3 ds, p, 3 ds, j to p of next ch, 3 ds, p, 3 ds, cl) 3 times, turn, ch 5 ds, 3 p sep by 2 ds, 5 ds, turn. Repeat from * around. Tie and cut.

SQUARE MEDALLION No. 27
(Two Shuttles)

Center motif: R 4 ds, 3 p sep by 4 ds, 4 ds, cl, (1-16-inch space), (r 4 ds, j to third p of last r, 4 ds, 2 p sep by 4 ds, 4 ds, cl, sp) 7 times, j last r to first r. Tie and cut. **1st row:** *R 6 ds, j to p of center motif, 6 ds, cl, turn, ch 4 ds, 3 p sep by 3 ds, 4 ds, turn, r 6 ds, j in same p with last r, 6 ds, cl, turn, ch 4 ds, 3 p sep by 3 ds, 4 ds, turn, r 6 ds, j to next p, 6 ds, cl, turn, ch 4 ds, 3 p sep by 3 ds, 4 ds, turn. Repeat from * around. Tie and cut. **2d row:** *R 4 ds, 3 p sep by 4 ds, 4 ds, cl, lr 4 ds, j in third p of last r, 4 ds, p, 4 ds, j in center p of ch between the two rings that are joined in same p on motif, 4 ds, 2 p sep by 4 ds, 4 ds, cl, r 4 ds, j to fifth p of lr, 4 ds, 2 p sep by 4 ds, 4 ds, cl, (turn, ch 2 ds, 7 p sep by 2 ds, 2 ds, turn, sr 6 ds, j in center p of next ch (last row), 6 ds, cl) 2 times, turn, ch 2 ds, 7 p sep by 2 ds, 2 ds. Repeat from * around. Tie and cut.

SQUARE MEDALLION No. 28
(Two Shuttles)

*Sr 4 ds, p, 4 ds, cl, lr 4 ds, j in p of sr, 4 ds, 2 p sep by 4 ds, 4 ds, cl, sr 4 ds, j in third p of lr, 4 ds, cl, turn, ch 8 ds, 2 p sep by 6 ds, 8 ds, repeat from * 4 times, j center p of each lr in p of first lr. Tie and cut. Make 3 more motifs, joining by the 2 picots on each side to form a square.

TATTED ROUND MEDALLION No. 29
(Two Shuttles)

R 3 ds, 3 p sep by 3 ds, 3 ds, cl, (sp (1-16-inch), r 3 ds, j to third p of last r, 3 ds, 2 p sep by 3 ds, 3 ds, cl) 5 times, j last r to first r. Tie and cut. **1st row:** Lr 3 ds, 2 p sep by 3 ds, 3 ds, j to p of center motif, 3 ds, 2 p sep by 3 ds, 3 ds, cl, turn, *r 7 p, cl, turn, ch 9 ds, turn, sr, 3 ds, j to fourth p of lr, 3 ds, 2 p sep by 3 ds, 3 ds, cl, sr 3 ds, 3 p sep by 3 ds, 3 ds, cl, turn, ch 9 ds, turn, lr 3 ds, p, 3 ds, j to third p of sr, 3 ds, j to next p on motif, 3 ds, 2 p sep by 3 ds, 3 ds, cl, repeat from * around. Tie and cut. **2d row:** *R 3 ds, p, 3 ds, j in center p of sr, 3 ds, p, 3 ds, cl, turn, ch 7 ds, 3 p sep by 2 ds, 7 ds, turn, r 3 ds, p, 3 ds, j in center p of sr, 3 ds, p, 3 ds, cl, turn, ch 7 ds, 3 p sep by 2 ds, 7 ds, turn, repeat from * around. Tie and cut.

DIRECTIONS FOR EDGINGS

(Continued from page 25)

EDGING No. 20
(Two Shuttles)

Medallions: (White) r 14 lp, cl, tie and cut. (Pink thread) r 5 ds, 5 p sep by 2 ds, 5 ds, cl, *sp (3/8-inch), sr 3 ds, j to lp of center ring, 3 ds, cl, sp, r 5 ds, j to last p of lr, 2 ds, 4 p sep by 2 ds, 5 ds, cl, repeat from * around, j to first lr. Tie and cut.
Make as many medallions as required, joining each to the other by center p of 2 rings on each medallion.
Make small motif as follows: R 5 ds, sk 2 rs from where the medallions are joined together, j in center p of next r, 3 ds, 4 p sep by 3 ds, 5 ds, cl, make 2 more rings, j second r to first r, and third r to second r, also to next r on medallion. Tie and cut. Make the small motif for each large medallion to form a scallop. **Edge:** *R 3 ds (pink), j to center p of r of medallion, 3 ds, cl, (white), ch 7 ds, p, 7 ds, repeat across top and down side of scallop to center r of small motif, j sr to 2 p of lr, and leave off the ch between 2 sr at intersection of points. Finish other scallops in same way.

SCARF ENDS No. 21
(Two Shuttles)

All rings are yellow and chains are white.
Motifs: R 12 p, cl, tie and cut. **1st row:** Sr 6 ds, j to p of center r, 6 ds, cl, *ch 8 ds, p, 8 ds, sr 6 ds, j to next p of center r, 6 ds, cl, repeat from * around, tie and cut. **2d row:** Sr 6 ds, j to p of last row, 6 ds, cl, *ch 8 ds, 3 p sep by 2 ds, 8 ds, sr 6 ds, j to next p of last row, 6 ds, cl, repeat from * around, tie and cut. Join each motif to the other by center p of 2 chs, of each motif. Make the small motif as follows: (yellow) r 6 ds, sk 1 ch from the connecting large motifs, j in center p of next ch, 2 ds, 4 p sep by 2 ds, 6 ds, cl, r 6 ds, j to last p of r, 2 ds, 4 p sep by 2 ds, 6 ds, cl, r 6 ds, j to p of last r, 2 ds, 3 p sep by 2 ds, 2 ds, j to center p of next ch, 6 ds, cl, tie and cut. Make a small motif on each large motif for a scallop. Make same motif, only join it to the chains so it will come between the two large motifs. Make one at each end, joining only one side to the large motif.
Outer Edge: Sr 6 ds, j in center p of first r in small motif at corner, 6 ds, cl, turn, ch 7 ds, 5 p sep by 2 ds, 7 ds, turn, r 6 ds, j in first p of next r of motif, 6 ds, cl, ch 7 ds, 5 p sep by 2 ds, 7 ds, r 6 ds, sk 1 p on same r, j in next p, 6 ds, cl, ch 7 ds, 5 p sep by 2 ds, 7 ds, r 6 ds, j in center p of next lr of motif, 6 ds, cl, *ch 7 ds, 5 p sep by 2 ds, 7 ds, r 6 ds, j to center p of ch on large motif, 6 ds, cl, repeat from * across top of motifs, joining each sr in center p each time. Work around next corner same as first corner, also each point of scallop in same manner. When ch is reached where the two large motifs are joined, j two small rings without a chain between them to the free ps of same joining chains.

Tatted Luncheon Set

For a luncheon set of 6 doilies and one runner, 11 balls of either STAR CROCHET COTTON or SILKINE CROCHET COTTON in size No. 10 are needed, and two shuttles.

MEDALLION

Make four small medallions for center of large medallion as follows: R 4 ds, 3 p sep by 4 ds, 4 ds, cl, (r 4 ds, j to third p of last r, 4 ds, 2 p sep by 4 ds, 4 ds, cl) 3 times, j each together by side p. **1st row:** *R 7 ds, j in corner p of center medallion, 7 ds, cl, ch 4 ds, 3 p sep by 4 ds, 4 ds, r 7 ds, j in same p with last r, 7 ds, cl, ch 4 ds, 3 p sep by 4 ds, 4 ds, r 7 ds, j in p between 2 small medallions, 7 ds, cl, ch 4 ds, 3 p sep by 4 ds, 4 ds. Repeat from * around. Tie and cut.

EDGE

R 4 ds, 3 p sep by 4 ds, 4 ds, cl, *ch 6 ds, p, 6 ds, r 7 ds, j to third p of last r, 7 ds, cl, (r 7 ds, p, 7 ds) twice, ch 6 ds, p, 6 ds, r 4 ds, j to p of last r, 4 ds, 2 p sep by 4 ds, 4 ds, cl. Repeat from * around.

To make the luncheon set: Cut the linen for the doilies to measure about 10¾ by 13¾ inches and the center to measure about 13¾ by 25¼ inches. Baste the medallions in place as shown, cut out the linen, allowing ³⁄₁₆ inch for turning under, baste this down, and cover with an over and over stitch. Turn a narrow hem, and sew the edging in place.